A Young Hunter's Guide to
Waterfowling and Conservation

Jim Spencer

Illustrations by Gary Cox

DUCKS
UNLIMITED

Memphis, Tennessee

Ducks Unlimited, Inc., and colophon are registered trademarks of Ducks Unlimited, Inc. One Waterfowl Way, Memphis, TN 38120.

Book design by Gary Cox

Published by Ducks Unlimited, Inc.
D. A. (Don) Young, Executive Vice President, Publisher

Published in cooperation with:
Ducks Unlimited Canada
P.O. Box 1160
Stonewall, MB, Canada R0C2Z0

ISBN: 1-932052-18-6
Published April 2004

Ducks Unlimited
Ducks Unlimited conserves, restores, and manages wetlands and associated habitats for North America's waterfowl. These habitats also benefit other wildlife and people.
    Since its founding in 1937, DU has raised more than $2 billion, which has contributed to the conservation of more than 11 million acres of prime wildlife habitat in all 50 states, each of the Canadian provinces, and in key areas of Mexico. In the U.S. alone, DU has helped to conserve over 2 million acres of waterfowl habitat. Some 900 species of wildlife live and flourish on DU projects, including many threatened and endangered species.

Call to Action
The success of Ducks Unlimited hinges upon each member's personal involvement in the conservation of North America's wetlands and waterfowl. You can help Ducks Unlimited meet its conservation goals by volunteering your time, energy, and resources; by participating in our conservation programs; and by encouraging others to do the same. To learn more about how you can make a difference for the ducks, in the U.S. call 1-800-45-DUCKS or vist the Web site www.ducks.org. In Canada call 1-800-665-DUCK or visit www.ducks.ca.

Distributed by The Globe Pequot Press, P.O. Box 480, Guilford, CT 06437-0480.

Library of Congress Cataloging-in-Publication Data

Spencer, Jim, 1947-
    A young hunter's guide to waterfowling and conservation / Jim Spencer ; illustrations by Gary Cox.
      p. cm.
    ISBN 1-932052-18-6 (alk. paper)
    1. Waterfowl shooting–Juvenile literature. I. Cox, Gary, 1957- ill. II. Title.
    SK331.S58 2004
    799.2'44--dc22

                          2004006026

Contents

Acknowledgments

Ducks Unlimited wishes to recognize Dr. Frank Baldwin for his vision and instructional programs for youth, which led to the development of this book. The editorial review and information provided by Dr. Baldwin, Dr. Rick Wishart, Dr. Henry Murkin, D. A. (Don) Young, and Eric Nuse are also gratefully acknowledged. Special thanks to Robert N. Corrigan Jr., Hazard K. Campbell, and Barry H. Martin for their funding support to initiate this project.

Introduction

Many of us were fortunate to grow up hunting ducks and geese. The pleasure of this outdoor experience is sometimes difficult to describe to the uninitiated. The wild wings in wild places, the enduring friendships, the bonds with family, the traditions, the seemingly never-ending array of gear, and of course the thrill of accomplishment under often adverse conditions are individual components of an overall experience that is so much more than the sum of its parts.

For those of you who are considering joining the ranks of duck and goose hunters or who are just getting started in the sport, we hope this book will provide you with a good foundation. The book focuses not only on gear and tactics but on all the elements of becoming a good waterfowl hunter. Developing an understanding of, and a respect for, your quarry is key. So, too, is discovering the rich history and traditions of the sport, and gaining insights into the future of waterfowl conservation and waterfowl hunting. Once you get started, you will develop your own set of skills and traditions that you will, we hope, pass on to friends and family members.

Ducks Unlimited's founders in 1937 were concerned hunters who realized the value of conservation work to the future of hunting—one of our most cherished traditions. Over the decades, Ducks Unlimited has carried out its mission of conservation—restoring and protecting wetland and upland habitats for the benefit of North America's waterfowl.

Hunters and others who enjoy the outdoors have raised more money for real, on-the-ground conservation projects than any other group. Through taxes on sporting equipment, duck stamps, contributions to private groups like DU, North America's hunters and anglers have raised billions of dollars to fund conservation work.

In turn, DU has provided this continent's hunters with a most important dividend: increasingly healthy populations of ducks, geese, and other wildlife. Wetlands and associated habitats are a magic ingredient in the recipe for duck production. But wetlands also mean cleaner water, less flooding, and places to hunt, fish, and enjoy the outdoors.

The people of DU have been passionate about their conservation mission. Many of those people are hunters; some are not. But more often than not, hunters and conservationists are one and the same. True hunters have a passion for wildlife. A passion for seeing ducks lighting, wings cupped, into a marsh. And a passion for protecting both the future of our natural resources and the future of our waterfowl hunting traditions.

We're proud to have the endorsement of the International Hunter Education Association and National Shooting Sports Foundation in helping to recruit the next generation of waterfowl hunters. Together, we hope this book will become a standard reference text and companion to other "getting started" tools such as hunter safety education courses and books.

D.A. (Don) Young
Executive Vice President
Ducks Unlimited, Inc.

Gordon Edwards
Executive Vice President
Ducks Unlimited Canada

Getting Started

Waterfowling Through the Ages

Hunting waterfowl is part of the heritage of people everywhere. The bones of wild ducks and geese have been found in archeological digs in Australia, New Zealand, northern Europe, South America, and practically everywhere else in the world.

In 1924, in Lovelock Cave in western Nevada, scientists found a set of primitive duck and goose decoys made of tightly bound grasses. These are the oldest known decoys in the world, dating back 1,800 to 2,000 years. No one knows when American Indians made and used the first duck decoys, but it's a pretty safe bet it was longer ago than that.

When the first European settlers arrived in North America, they found American Indians using decoys much like the ones found in Lovelock Cave. The Indians didn't have firearms, so they used the decoys to lure ducks and geese within range of their bows, slings, nets, traps, and snares.

At first, the newly arrived Europeans didn't pay much attention to the plentiful ducks and geese. Lead and gunpowder were scarce and expensive, and it made more sense to shoot a moose, elk, bear, or deer because there was so much more meat on these animals. A duck or goose was too small to justify the expense of shooting it.

But as more and more settlers came, big game got scarce. Hunters turned their attention to ducks and geese, and guess what? They quickly learned, as the American Indians had known for thousands of years, that decoys were a big help in attracting waterfowl. They also learned that ducks and geese were nutritious and tasty, and that waterfowl hunting can be fun and challenging.

The equipment used by modern duck hunters is much different from that used by American Indians and the early European settlers. Today's technology has given us space-age materials to help keep us warm and dry, and modern firearms and ammunition have made us more efficient and effective hunters.

One thing, though, hasn't changed. Waterfowl hunting is as enjoyable and as exciting in the 21st century as it was for the hunter who hid those grass decoys in Lovelock Cave nearly 2,000 years ago. Such is the rich tradition and special bond today's young hunters share with other waterfowlers throughout the ages.

Individual Responsibilities

Although there are many more nonhunters than hunters these days, it's got more to do with lack of opportunity than lack of interest. People who live in cities often lose touch with their hunting heritage and the natural world. Surveys have shown that most people support waterfowl hunting when it is done in an ethical manner. To maintain that support, it is important that you remember that hunting is a privilege and a serious responsibility. If only a few of us act poorly, all of us pay the price.

Here are a few things all hunters should do:

- Enroll in a hunter education course. All states and provinces offer classes in hunter safety, and everyone who wants to become a waterfowler has the opportunity and obligation to learn the fundamentals of safe firearms handling and careful hunting practices taught in these courses. You can check on the availability of such courses in your area by contacting your state or provincial conservation department or the International Hunter Education Association (IHEA) at www.ihea.com. The National Shooting Sports Foundation (NSSF) is another leading advocate of firearms safety and hunter education, and offers safety literature for children, teens, and adults at www.nssf.org.

- Learn to identify waterfowl. This is both a legal and an ethical obligation. Different species of ducks and geese have different bag limits, so you must know what you are shooting at before you shoot. While there is no substitute for observing live ducks and geese in the field, you should consult waterfowl books, identification guides, or posters even before you go hunting. In the process you will not only become a more ethical hunter, but a better hunter as well.

- Obey all game laws. Hunting regulations are there to protect wildlife populations and keep them from being overhunted. Never take more than the legal limit, and don't hunt in an illegal fashion, such as hunting over bait. Don't shoot before or after legal shooting hours. Don't hunt out of season. Make sure of your target before shooting, since some species of ducks and geese are protected by more restrictive regulations. Poachers are people who knowingly break game laws for their own benefit or profit and in the process hurt the image of hunting. Don't be one of them. Many states and provinces operate a program to report poachers. Become familiar with the program in your area and see how you can become a supporter.

• Show respect for landowners and their property. Never hunt on private land without permission. And once you have obtained permission, be a good guest. Leave farm gates as you found them. Don't litter, bother livestock, or cross standing crops or muddy field roads and make deep ruts. In short, treat the land the way you'd want someone to treat it if you were the landowner.

• Respect other hunters. If another group gets to your planned hunting spot first, give it up and try somewhere else. For everyone's safety and enjoyment don't set up close to another group of hunters and don't intercept birds that are working someone else's decoys. Give your fellow hunter the benefit of the doubt and don't argue about who shot what bird. A good rule of thumb is to stay at least a quarter mile apart from other waterfowling groups. Many public areas are crowded with hunters, and courteous behavior makes the experience better for everyone.

• Work on your shooting skills to reduce your chances of wounding and losing birds. Likewise, avoid shooting at birds that are beyond the effective range of the loads and chokes you are using. (See chapter 6 for more details on shotguns, chokes, and patterns.)

• Learn, too, how to estimate distances by using a range finder or a process called "subtending," which will help you judge the size of the bird you are shooting at compared to the size of the muzzle of your shotgun (again, see chapter 6). Always shoot within the limits of your own personal skills. And whenever possible, shoot at single birds rather than at flocks or groups of birds.

- Choose hunting sites that will allow you to set up your shot so that the birds fall into open areas instead of heavy cover, where they can become lost or impossible to retrieve. If a bird flies over heavy cover, avoid taking the shot.

- Always keep your eyes on shot birds so you can mark where they fall. And be sure to use a trained retriever to help you find and retrieve all fallen birds. If you do lose a bird, it's a good idea to count that one against your daily bag limit.

- Take going-away shots only when the birds are within 30 yards from you. And use "swatter" loads (see chapter 6) to kill wounded birds on the water.

- Make every effort to retrieve all downed game, whether wounded or dead, as soon as possible. It's the law. Losing crippled or dead ducks is sometimes unavoidable, but make every effort to retrieve everything you shoot. If a duck or goose is still alive when you retrieve it, kill it as quickly and humanely as possible.

- Don't waste game. If you shoot it, you have a responsibility to make use of it.

- Give ducks and geese a sporting chance. Always treat wildlife with respect and with wise use in mind.

There are many other things that could be included in this chapter, but you're probably getting the idea. Treat other hunters and landowners like you want to be treated. Everyone will be better off—and so will the future of hunting for those who come after you.

Clothing and Equipment

Clothing and gear are important for waterfowling, but you don't need a huge pile of it to get started. The important thing is to have personal gear that will keep you warm, dry, and safe.

If you're planning to sneak up on a few farm ponds and jump-shoot ducks, you might need nothing more than a shotgun, a few shells, and clothing that's suitable for the weather. Other kinds of waterfowl hunting require more equipment, some of it quite expensive. For a hunt on a big lake or open marsh, for example, you might need a boat, motor, a large number of decoys, chest waders, a portable or permanent blind, and a lot of other stuff besides. Probably your best bet here is to find an experienced hunter who already has the gear and will introduce you to this style of hunting.

Clothing Makes the Duck Hunter

Fall and winter weather are fickle. Early mornings are usually chilly to cold, but by midday temperatures are often mild or even warm. On top of that, the weather can change in a matter of minutes, and a dry, mild, sunny day can become a wet, cold, miserable one almost before you know it's happening.

The best way to deal with these varying conditions is by layering your clothing. Start with a set of long underwear next to the skin (polypropylene

The best way to deal with varying conditions is by layering your clothing.

does a great job of keeping you warm and wicking away sweat; wool or silk are also effective), followed by a wool or synthetic fleece shirt and a pair of comfortable pants. Top this off with a nylon or Gore-Tex layer. Avoid wearing anything cotton, which absorbs water and keeps moisture close to your skin, cooling you even further.

Over all of this, wear a pair of insulated coveralls, or bib overalls with a medium-weight waterfowl jacket. Bring a pair of insulated and waterproof gloves. A second pair of lightweight glove liners or half-finger gloves is also a good idea for milder conditions and will make it easy to shoot your gun. Heavy rubber gloves are useful if you'll be working with wet decoys. A baseball-style cap is adequate for most fall hunting, but later in the season when the weather is colder a camo-colored ski mask or a hat with drop-down earflaps will help keep you warmer.

On a day without rain, dressing this way will allow you to stay comfortable down to temperatures well below freezing. You can remove layers or put them back on to match whatever conditions the weather brings.

Rain is for the Birds

Hunting is often best during the worst weather. Ducks and geese move around more when the weather is bad, and they decoy better and seem less wary. Maybe this is because they can't see as well in bad weather, or maybe it's because they're trying to find a sheltered spot. Probably it's a combination of those and possibly other factors.

Your challenge is to stay warm and dry in these conditions. If you're wet, the temperature doesn't have to be very low to make you miserable.

Plastic or rubber ponchos were popular for a long time, and they're still sold today. They're economical and easy to carry. If you're going to be sitting still in an open boat or blind, where you can arrange the loose-fitting poncho over you to keep you dry, these garments are still a fair choice. But they don't "breathe" well, trapping your body moisture inside so you end up a little damp anyway. Most ponchos are fairly flimsy, too, and they're easy to rip and tear.

The best rainwear for the waterfowl hunter is a jacket made of Gore-Tex or other similar breathable waterproof fabric. These jackets and parkas come in uninsulated or insulated styles for use in mild or cold weather. Get one that has a hood. A waterfowl coat should be long enough to cover your seat and hips if you don't plan to wear waders. Otherwise a hip-length coat will do. A hunter wearing one of these coats is almost as waterproof as the ducks themselves.

Footwear

For jump-shooting ponds and shallow creeks, knee-high rubber boots may be enough. But you will need some sort of waders for most duck hunting.

Hip waders are often suitable for hunting small potholes or flooded fields. Hip waders cover your legs from the hips down and have straps on the tops that snap onto your belt or belt loops.

Many waterfowl hunters choose chest waders—waders that come nearly up to your armpits. These have several advantages. First, they add one more layer of insulation between you and the air, so they're warmer. They also

See the Marsh, Be the Marsh

Every hunting catalog these days has page after page of camouflage gear. Some of it is so realistic you'd swear they pasted leaves and grass right on the fabric.

Camouflage clothing has been invented to imitate marsh grass, wooded forests, flooded backwaters, and nearly every other place ducks and geese are found.

Do you need to own this super-realistic clothing to hunt ducks and geese successfully? Although the modern camouflage patterns are very effective, hunters have been making do for many years with drab green and brown clothing that blends in with the natural plants around them.

The important thing is to fade into the background as best you can. A camouflage hat is a good idea to cover your head, and a camouflage face net or camouflage face paint will take the bright shine off your skin.

Once you find out where you like to hunt the most, you can start saving your money for a realistic camouflage outfit that matches your surroundings.

help keep you dry when it rains. Chest waders let you wade deeper water than hip waders, but they are handy for hunting in shallower water, as well. You can sit down in a shallow puddle or sit on a wet stump or log and stay dry. Chest waders can also help you stay dry when you trip and fall in shallow water—something that eventually happens to every duck hunter in the world.

Chest waders are also heavier and they cost more. You don't have to buy the most expensive waders in the catalog, but don't buy anything that looks cheap or flimsy. These "bargains" often don't last through even one hunt. It's also a good idea to wear a wading belt, which will keep your waders from flooding if you happen to step into water that's over the top of your waders.

Other Equipment

Here is a list of items you may need on your duck hunting trips. But you don't have to run out and buy them all. The mentor or adult you hunt with may own many of them. Others you may want to add as you need them, and as you can afford them.

Handwarmers. There are two types: One type is a metal case you fill with lighter fluid or solid fuel. The other is a plastic pouch that gets warm when taken out of the airtight package and shaken. They both work. The plastic pouches are the easiest to use.

Heater. A propane heater is a useful item for boat or blind hunting in severely cold weather, but can be a fire hazard and can produce poisonous fumes if used in a poorly ventilated place. A catalytic heater may be a good alternative.

Flotation gear. This is a must for any type of duck hunting that involves using a boat. Wear a Coast-Guard-approved PFD (Personal Flotation Device) whenever you are in the boat.

Compass or GPS unit. This isn't necessary for hunting a small lake or pond, but it can mean the difference between safety and disaster on big water or in flooded woods. These items can also be useful in making your way back to a hard-to-find hunting spot.

Fire-starting kit. You can make a simple one with a three-inch piece of candle, an aspirin bottle full of wooden waterproof matches, a partial roll of toilet paper, and a small plastic container of charcoal starter fluid, all stored in a resealable plastic baggy.

First-aid kit. A commercial kit is fine, but you can assemble your own in a small fishing tackle box. Include aspirin, tweezers, a small pair of scissors, several sizes of bandages, antiseptic, sterile gauze, and a roll of first-aid tape.

Other items you—or your hunting companion—may want to bring on a waterfowl outing include: waterproof flashlight, whistle, binoculars, duct tape, thermos of hot drink or soup, energy bars, tide tables, waterfowl regulations, sunset tables, and a bucket or fold-out seat.

Talk to the Experts

Before outfitting yourself for a waterfowl hunt, try to talk with mentors or other hunters who are familiar with conditions in the area you're hunting. Local sporting goods stores are reliable sources of information. Ask them what they think is the necessary equipment for the type of hunting you plan on doing. That way, you'll probably have everything you need and you won't be burdened with a lot of unnecessary equipment.

Scouting Before the Hunt

Ducks and geese are often on the move. They migrate from north to south in fall and south to north the following spring. They also move from place to place while they're in a particular state, province, or territory. A marsh or lake that has plenty of ducks this week might have few or no ducks next week.

The main reasons ducks move from place to place are to find food, open water, or shelter. Waterfowl won't stay long in a place that doesn't have two or more of these elements. That's why it is important to scout your territory before you go hunting.

History Can Help, But Not Always

Conditions change from one duck season to the next, and the marsh where you and your hunting partner did so well last season may be dry and duckless this year. If that's the case, it's good to know beforehand, so you won't waste a valuable hunting day going to a place that doesn't have any birds.

On the other hand, the past history of a hunting area is a good indicator of how productive it will be this year if there is still an adequate supply of water and food nearby. If you or someone you know has had good luck at a particular marsh, pothole, or goose field, by all means check it out. Just don't become so hung up on an old favorite spot that you waste your time there, even though the conditions have changed and it's not as good this year.

It's a good idea to get out to the marsh, pothole, or goose field well before the season starts. Whenever possible, go with a seasoned hunter or birder. These veterans of the outdoors can help you identify a variety of ducks and geese, by sight and by sound, and you'll learn better and faster through their guidance than you would on your own.

You'll learn a lot, too, if you purchase a handy field guide or ID book with color illustrations or photos of waterfowl. Carry it with you in the field, along with a pair of binoculars, and practice identifying all the waterfowl you see.

Chapter 12, "The Basics of Waterfowling Biology," will give you a nice start at understanding ducks and geese. And the "Suggested Readings" section at the end of the book offers a number of excellent reference books that will help you learn even more about waterfowl, which in turn will help you become a better hunter.

Let Your Fingers Do the Walking

By far the best way to scout is to get out there and take a firsthand look at your hunting area. That may not be possible if the place you plan to hunt is a long way from home. In that case, maps can be a great help.

Topographical maps (usually called topo maps) are the best types of maps for scouting. These maps show the natural features of the land such as streams, woodlands, marshes, potholes, lakes, and ponds. They also show changes in altitude. By using these maps before you go into the field, you can locate low marshy areas, creeks, and other waters where ducks might be found.

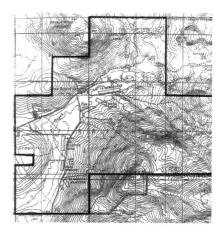

But topo maps are expensive, and they're awkward to use in the field because they're susceptible to water damage and they blow around in the wind. You can also buy a CD of topo maps for your area from companies such as DeLorme, ToposUSA, and others. You can order these on the Internet from several Web sites, such as www.delorme.com, www.maptown.com, and www.fedpubs.com.

Rely on Other Sources

State and provincial/territorial conservation agencies, public hunting area headquarters, and sporting goods shops are also good places to get information regarding water and food conditions and duck numbers and locations. The people at these kinds of places want you to have good hunting, and the information they give you will usually be reliable.

Don't be afraid to talk to the people who own the land, too; if anyone knows where the wetlands and the waterfowl are, it's the people who live nearby. Once the season opens, you will need the permission of landowners to hunt anyway, so start early and get to know these folks. Maintaining friendships with landowners and respecting their property rights are sure-fire ways to find good places to hunt year after year.

Network With Your Hunting Buddies

Duck hunters don't like to talk much about their best hunting spots. They guard this information very carefully because too many hunters in an area can ruin the experience for everyone.

If you have close friends who hunt ducks, however, chances are they will be glad to share information with you. If you know the up-to-date conditions on Lake Wobegon and your buddy knows what's going on at Lake Can'tFindIt, you can pool your information and both of you will be better off.

It's best to keep this circle of friends fairly small. Sharing information with two or three other hunters is fine, but if you're swapping information with fifty other hunters, you might find yourself in a crowd when you go out on opening day.

Young hunters should try to find an older, knowledgeable person who can act as a teacher or mentor. Such elder statesmen are proud of what they know and are often willing to take a rookie under their wing and pass along their experience and a few of their secrets.

Sources of topo maps:

U.S. Geological Survey
12201 Sunrise Valley Drive
Reston, VA 20192, USA
http://mapping.usgs.gov/

Natural Resources Canada
615 Booth Street, Room 711
Ottawa, Ontario, Canada
K1A 0E9
Telephone: 1-800-465-6277
Fax: (613) 947-7948
E-Mail: topo.maps@NRCan.gc.ca

Going Hunting

Safety on the Hunt

Waterfowl hunters get up early, and they go outside in the dark and in the cold. They stay out when the weather turns nasty. They ride in boats on rough water. They wade in cold water where the footing is tricky. They carry shotguns.

All these activities can be dangerous. That's why it's important for waterfowl hunters to always keep safety in mind before, during, and after the hunt. By following a few common-sense safety rules, you can keep your hunts exciting and enjoyable, and prevent them from turning unpleasant or even tragic.

Firearms safety is discussed in chapter 7. It's a very important part of being safe while hunting, but there's a lot more to safe hunting than just watching where your gun is pointing.

Hope for the Best, but Prepare for the Worst

Even if the weather is mild when you begin a hunt, fall and winter weather can change fast. If you're wearing light clothes when a cold front moves through, you're in for a miserable time. Remember, too, it's usually colder and windier near the water. Dress in layers, as we discussed in chapter 3, and carry a warm, waterproof coat or parka with a hood. If the weather is mild you can use it as a seat cushion. If things turn nasty, it can be a lifesaver.

Planning Prevents Problems

Thinking ahead before you go hunting is the best way to avoid trouble. Is the weather going to be cold? Bundle up. Is the water going to be deep? Wear chest waders or hunt from the boat. Are you going to an unfamiliar place? Take a map and compass or GPS unit.

Always let somebody else know where you're going and when you expect to return home. This is important whether you are hunting near home or far away. If something goes wrong, it helps enormously to have someone looking for you.

You may think that it sounds like too much trouble to take all these precautions. If so, that's because you're reading it while you're warm and dry and comfortable. That should be your goal as a waterfowl hunter—to stay warm and dry and comfortable.

And safe.

Hypothermia Kills

A combination of wind, wet clothes, and low temperatures can kill you. It happens through a process called hypothermia. The cold wind and wet clothes suck heat out of your body faster than your body can make more heat to replace it. Your body temperature begins to fall and you begin to shiver uncontrollably. A drop of only a degree or two in core body temperature causes problems with coordination and mental capacity, and accidents are more likely to happen. As the body temperature falls even lower, you become confused and sleepy. With hypothermia, it's a sleep from which many people never wake.

The best way to prevent hypothermia is to stay well clothed and dry and keep out of the wind. Wear clothing that will wick water away from your skin. That's simple enough, but what if you or someone in your hunting party gets chilled and hypothermia begins?

Symptoms of Hypothermia

Hypothermia doesn't happen all at once, but in stages that worsen as the body cools. Mental symptoms appear first and may include feeling "fuzzy headed" or unable to think clearly, feeling tired and "out of it," and slurring your words—as if your tongue won't work properly. Physical symptoms come next and may include shivering, goose bumps, clumsiness, and stiffness.

Warm 'Em Up Quick

In all cases of hypothermia, the first thing to do is to prevent further heat loss. Get the affected person out of the weather as quickly and completely as possible. If you can't get the victim inside, at least get him or her out of the wind. Get in a wind-tight emergency shelter (see page 24). Build a fire and get the victim's wet clothes off, if possible, and either replace them with dry clothes or dry the victim's wet clothes by the fire while keeping the victim warm. Put the victim in a sleeping bag or wrap him in blankets if possible. Movement, rubbing, shivering, and foot stamping will get the circulation going and produce more heat.

Give the victim warm (not hot) liquids, such as water, milk, or soup. Foods high in carbohydrates like bread or pasta, release quickly into the bloodstream and provide a sudden brief surge of heat. Do NOT give a hypothermia victim alcohol or drinks high in caffeine, which lead to increased heat loss or dehydration.

Again, the most important thing is to keep the victim from getting any colder. In mild to moderate cases of hypothermia, once the victim has gotten warm again, there are rarely any lingering side effects. In severe cases, however, hypothermia can prove life threatening. So get the victim to help as soon as possible.

Emergency Shelters

In a pinch, duck blinds and overturned boats can be used as emergency shelters. You can also use a tarp, poncho, garbage bags, or ground cloth to make an emergency shelter to protect against wind, rain, and snow. Keep the covering as low to the ground as possible to reduce wind resistance, and use rocks, logs, or other heavy objects to hold it down. Tie the upper corners securely to stout bushes or trees, and run the cover around several trees or bushes, if possible, to make it more wind resistant. Cattails, reed grass, or other dry vegetation can also be used as bedding.

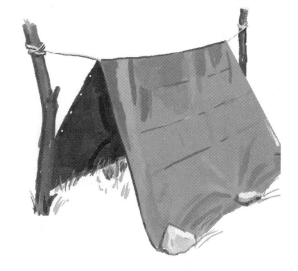

Handy Emergency Gear You Hope You'll Never Need

The fire-starting kit and first-aid kit mentioned in chapter 3 are a good start for emergency gear. Here are a few more items to consider carrying:

Flashlight and extra batteries. A flashlight is useful for helping you get to your hunting site before first light. And you'll need it again if you get caught out after dark.

Emergency flare. Use it to summon help if you get lost, or to start a fire in wet conditions.

Emergency blanket. A lightweight, inexpensive cover that can keep you warm or protect you from the sun's rays.

Map and compass or GPS unit. The purpose of these items is obvious, but be sure you know how to use them before you have to rely on them to get you out of trouble.

Cellular telephone. A good thing to have if you're hunting in an area where you can get a signal to send and receive calls. If not, it's as worthless as a rock.

Quick-energy snack food. Granola bars, chocolate, raisins, trail mix. To make sure these foods are available for emergency use, keep a small stash separate from the normal snack food you take on a duck hunt. Don't dip into your emergency stash except in a true emergency, or one day when you really need it, it won't be there.

Other food. Canned meat, peanut butter, apples, oranges. These emergency rations should also be kept separate from the normal lunch food for your hunt and used only in real emergency situations.

First-aid handbook. Take a course in wilderness first aid and bring along a pocket handbook on the subject to help you out in times of emergency.

About Shotguns

Waterfowl hunting today is done with a *shotgun*. A shotgun is designed to shoot a shell that contains many small round pellets called *shot*, instead of one large bullet, as does a rifle. Each shotgun shell contains many of these shot pellets—a 12-gauge shell, for example, may have one hundred pellets or more.

A shotgun is meant to be accurate on small or fast-moving targets at short distances. To hit a target, the shotgun shooter depends on these shot spreading into a wider arrangement called a *pattern*. The pattern gets larger as it moves away from the barrel of the gun.

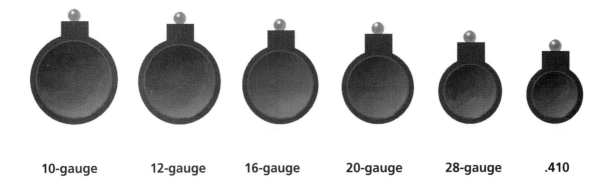

10-gauge   12-gauge   16-gauge   20-gauge   28-gauge   .410

Shotgun Gauges

The size of most shotguns is stated by *gauge*. There are six gauges of shotguns still in use today—10, 12, 16, 20, 28, and .410. Of the six, the two most commonly used for waterfowl are 12-gauge and 20-gauge.

The smaller the gauge number, the larger the *bore*—the hole in the barrel through which the shot passes. For example, a 10-gauge shotgun has a larger bore than a 12-gauge, and a 12-gauge bore is larger than a 20-gauge. This is true for all shotgun sizes except the .410, the bore of which is measured in decimal parts of an inch.

Because larger shotguns have a larger bore, the shells that fit those bores will hold more shot pellets and gunpowder. The largest legal shotgun for hunting in North America is the 10-gauge, but the most popular size for duck and goose hunters is the 12-gauge. There are more choices of brands, models, and styles in 12-gauge guns and ammunition, and both guns and ammo are easier to find for the 12 than for other gauges.

Many hunters (especially young people or those of smaller stature) use the considerably smaller, lighter, and easier-on-the-shoulder 20-gauge.

Shotgun Actions

Shotguns come in a variety of styles, or actions. The simplest, and the one many hunters start with, is the single-shot gun. It has a *break action*, which means that you press a lever and the gun hinges open in the middle so you can load a shell in the barrel. Then it snaps shut. Other break-action shotguns have two barrels. Like the names indicate, the *over-under* has one barrel on top of the other, and the *side-by-side* has two barrels beside each other.

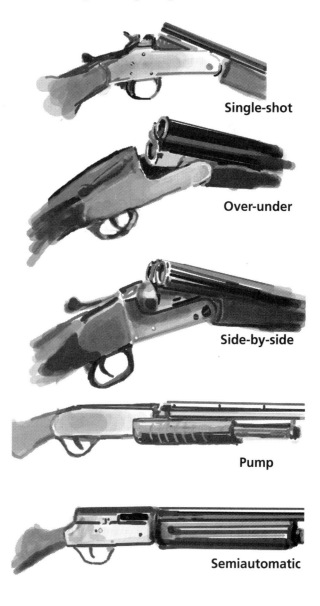

Single-shot

Over-under

Side-by-side

Pump

Semiautomatic

Other actions include the *pump-action* gun, which has a single barrel and inserts a new shell after each shot when you pull back on the forward grip, called the *fore-end*. The *semiautomatic* shotgun inserts a new shell each time you fire the gun, and you don't have to pull back on the fore-end. The extra shells are held in the gun's magazine.

Important note: Because semiautos and pumps often hold five or more shells, you'll need a wooden or plastic magazine plug, which will decrease the number of shells your gun will hold to the legal limit of three for waterfowl hunting.

Shot Sizes

Ducks and geese come in many sizes. A green-winged teal is the size of a pigeon, while a giant Canada goose can weigh as much as an adult turkey. It's no surprise, then, that goose hunters need heavier, harder-hitting ammunition than teal hunters.

Shot sizes, from the largest to the smallest, are: T, BBB, BB, 1, 2, 3, 4, 5, 6, 7½, 8, 9. The larger shot sizes are best when shooting at longer ranges, and smaller shot sizes are best for close-range shooting.

The size of the birds being hunted should also be considered when selecting your shot. The most popular goose loads are BBB, BB, and 1. Hunters shooting at giant Canada geese might need BBB shot or even larger. But snow goose hunters are better served by BB or 1 shot because the birds are smaller. Most duck hunters use 1, 2, 3, or 4 shot. Mallard hunters need larger shot than teal hunters or wood duck hunters, because the birds they're after are bigger.

| T | BBB | BB | 1 | 2 | 3 | 4 | 5 | 6 | 7½ | 8 | 9 |

Packing a Punch

The distance the shot will travel from a shotgun depends on two things—the size of the shot and how fast it's going when it leaves the barrel. Larger shot is heavier, and therefore has more momentum and travels farther. Fast-moving shot also has more momentum, and it travels farther than slower-moving shot of the same size.

Neither of those things has anything to do with the size of the shotgun. Even the tiny .410 shotgun will shoot just as far as the heaviest 10-gauge, as long as the same size shot is used and the speed of the pellets is the same.

But a 10-gauge shotgun will still consistently kill ducks and geese much farther away than a .410, and the reason is simple. The 10-gauge shell holds nearly four times as many shot pellets as the .410, and each pellet has the same energy. A load from the 10-gauge will put approximately four times as many pellets into the same target. So, the total amount of energy hitting the bird is much greater with the larger gun since more pellets are going to find the target.

Steel and Other Types of Nontoxic Shot

For many years all waterfowl hunters used *lead shot*. But several years ago research showed that lead shot from fired shotgun shells settled to the bottom of lakes and marshes, and when the shot was picked up by feeding ducks or other birds, the birds often died or were weakened by lead poisoning. As a result, laws in the United States and Canada now require waterfowl hunters to use only shot that is not toxic to birds. This *nontoxic shot* is now used in place of lead for waterfowl hunting.

At first, the only nontoxic shot available was steel shot. Today, in addition to steel, there are other nontoxic shot alternatives, including bismuth, tungsten-iron, tungsten-polymer, tungsten-matrix, tungsten-nickel-iron, and others. Different manufacturers give them different trade names, but each box of shells will indicate whether it contains nontoxic shot or not. All of these alternatives to steel shot are suitable for waterfowling because they are close or more similar to lead in density. They are also all more expensive, so most duck and goose hunters continue to use steel shot.

Chokes

Most shotgun barrels are not the same diameter from one end to the other. In most cases, the *muzzle* (the end of the shotgun farthest from you when you are shooting) is slightly smaller than the *breech* (the end of the barrel closest to you). The difference isn't much, usually only a few thousandths of an inch, but it's important.

This slight constriction at the muzzle is built into the gun to help the gun throw a tighter pattern of shot pellets. This is called the gun's *choke*. Guns with more choke fire smaller, tighter patterns, and guns with less choke throw wider, more open patterns. The common chokes, from the most open to the tightest, are called cylinder, improved-cylinder, modified, and full. Many guns now have *screw-in chokes* that let you change the choke for different hunting situations.

A gun that throws a tighter pattern will kill ducks and geese farther away than a gun with a more open choke. That's true, but only if the shot pattern hits the bird.

For most duck hunters, an improved-cylinder choke is the best choice. This choke gives an acceptably dense pattern with steel shot out to 35 or 40 yards. At the same time, it allows the pattern to expand and helps hunters who aren't good shots hit more of the ducks they shoot at.

Goose hunters, because of the bigger birds and often longer shooting ranges, may need a little more choke constriction, but modified choke is usually the right choice.

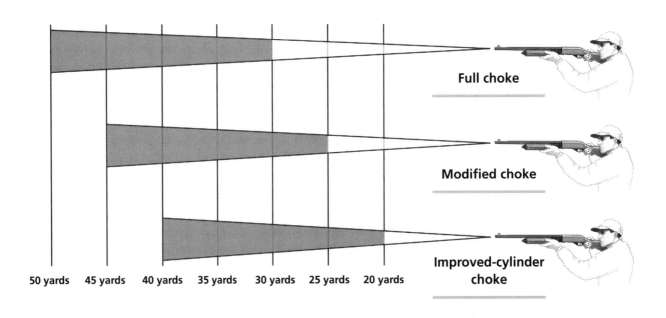

50 yards   45 yards   40 yards   35 yards   30 yards   25 yards   20 yards

Close-Range Tool

No matter how tight the choke, no matter how large the shot, no matter how dense the pattern, a shotgun is basically a close-range tool. If the duck or goose you're shooting at is much beyond 40 yards, it's not close enough to shoot at. No matter what.

Sure, you might hit a bird at that range or farther. You might even kill it cleanly if you're exceptionally lucky that day. But usually you'll miss, and that's the best of the things that can happen. Because sometimes you don't miss. A pellet or two finds its way to the target, but the bird isn't hit hard enough to bring it down.

It may, however, be hit hard enough that it won't survive the experience, in which case you've managed to cause prolonged and unnecessary suffering for a wild creature and wasted a valuable natural resource. Remember, you must make every effort to retrieve a wounded bird as soon as possible.

You can do your best to minimize crippling losses by practicing your shooting and learning to shoot as accurately as possible. You can also make sure you use the proper guns, shot sizes, and chokes. The best way to do this is to take your gun to a target range and test a variety of chokes and loads at distances of 25, 30, 35, and 40 yards. Draw a 30-inch circle on paper targets and aim for the center of the circle. The more pellets you put in the circle, the better. Look for dense, consistent patterns to tell you which chokes and loads work best at which distances.

Here are some general guidelines for hunting waterfowl with steel loads:

Situation/Range	Load	Shot Size	Suggested Choke
Small ducks over decoys up to 40 yards	1 to 1$\frac{1}{8}$ oz.	6 to 4	Improved-cylinder, modified
Medium to large ducks over decoys up to 40 yards	1 to $\frac{1}{4}$ oz.	4 to 2	Improved-cylinder, modified
Medium to large geese over decoys up to 45 yards	1$\frac{1}{8}$ to 1$\frac{9}{16}$ oz.	2 to BBB	Improved-cylinder, modified

Note: For wounded birds use 1-ounce "swatter" loads in sizes 7 to 5 with a modified choke.

Most important, know your limitations and have the willpower to not shoot at ducks and geese that are too far away.

Estimating Distances

And how will you know when waterfowl are too far away? You can measure distances with a range finder, an electronic device that will, for example, tell you the distance to the top of the trees across from your blind, and thus the relative distance of ducks flying over them. You can learn to judge distances without a range finder, as well, by using your own two eyes.

One of the best ways to do this is through a process called "subtending." You don't have to remember the word, just remember that it involves comparing the size of a bird to the size of your shotgun muzzle. Simply set up life-sized duck and goose decoys at 20-, 30-, and 40-yard distances, and see how much of the bird your gun muzzle covers at those distances. Practice this when you practice your target shooting, well before the hunting season, and by opening day it will become almost second nature. You'll be able to point your gun at a bird and determine quickly whether or not the bird is in range.

The farther away a bird is, the smaller it will appear in relation to your shotgun muzzle.

The Basics of Wingshooting

Safety Always

Proper wingshooting begins and ends with safe gun handling. The rules are simple, but important:

- Always be aware of where your gun is pointing. At a firing range, keep the muzzle pointed downrange at all times. When hunting, make sure you never point the gun in the direction of a person or pet, or at human property.
- Keep the safety on until the instant before you're ready to fire. Take your safety off as you're mounting the gun—not before.
- Regardless of whether or not you shoot, put the safety back on immediately after you've dismounted the gun.

35

- Get in the habit of checking every few minutes to make sure the safety is on. But remember, the only completely safe gun is an unloaded gun.
- Never lean a loaded gun against a vehicle, tree, fence, or other object. It could fall and discharge.
- Always unload a firearm when crossing a fence or ditch or when passing it to another person.
- Never assume a gun is unloaded. Check it to make sure. Work the action. Look in the chamber. Do this each time you put a gun in a case, car, or gun safe. Check it again when you remove it from these places.
- Regularly check your action and muzzle to make sure they are clear of obstructions.
- Make sure your ammunition is the correct gauge and size for your gun.
- Clean and maintain your gun after every use to keep it in smooth and safe working order.
- Always store your gun and ammunition separately in safe and locked locations.
- Never point a gun at anything you don't intend to shoot. It's not a toy; shooting is a serious activity.

Field Safety

In addition to the above firearms safety practices and those you learn in your hunter education course, there are a number of special safety rules for waterfowlers.

One of the most important is establishing safe zones of fire.

Generally, a safe zone of fire is an area into which you can shoot safely. When you're hunting alone, this area maybe defined by your field of view, the presence of unsuitable targets, and the range of your shotgun. When hunting with others, however, your safe zone of fire will usually be a 45° angle directly in front of you. This is especially true if you are hunting in the center of a blind, pit, or boat with other hunters on either side of you. The hunters on your left and right will have broader zones of fire since they can swing to the outside.

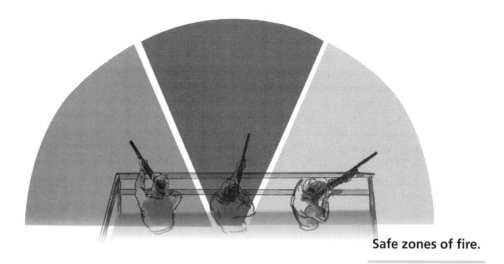

Safe zones of fire.

When hunting in a blind, pit, or boat you will be directly in line with and very close to your fellow hunters. So establishing safe zones of fire and abiding by them is critical. Do so right away, as soon as you take your positions in the blind, pit, or boat. Do it before you load your shotgun.

Hunting so close to your partners means you'll also need to establish rules about shooting order. In a small boat or blind, for example, it's often best if only one or two hunters fire at a time. Likewise, when the hunters rise to take the shot, the other hunters should remain seated and out the line of fire. Make sure everyone knows the shooting order and follows it religiously. As an extra precaution, call all of the shots in advance—"It's your shot, Jim"—just to be safe.

Precautions must be taken when carrying guns in and out of boats and blinds as well. Always make sure your gun is unloaded, the action open, before entering or exiting a boat, blind, or pit. If you are hunting with a partner, have your partner enter the boat or blind first, then hand him or her the unloaded gun or guns. When hunting alone, put the unloaded gun in the blind first before entering yourself. In a boat, place the gun (muzzle pointing forward) in the bow of the boat before getting in. A second hunter should place his gun in the stern with the muzzle pointing backwards before climbing in himself.

Be careful, too, about loading and unloading guns in the blind or boat. Always make sure the muzzle is pointed outside the blind or boat in a safe direction. Likewise, never rest your gun against the side of the blind or pit. Place it in a proper gun rest or hold it with the muzzle pointed in a safe direction.

Form Is Important

As mentioned in chapter 6, a shotgun and a rifle are different. A shotgun throws many pellets at once, and pinpoint accuracy isn't as important because the large pattern of shot compensates for the lack of precise aim. The rifle throws one bullet at a time and depends on pinpoint accuracy. That's why a rifle has sights, but a shotgun usually doesn't.

With a shotgun, your eyes are the rear "sight." The front "sight" is the end of your shotgun barrel.

Keep both eyes open when you're wingshooting with a shotgun. You need both eyes (this is called *binocular vision*) for depth perception and to give you a better sight picture between the gun and the target.

To hit a moving target with a shotgun, you line up your eyes, the end of the barrel, and the target.

As your eyes are the rear sight of the shotgun, to line them up properly on the target you must be looking along the gun barrel, rather than looking down on it from a higher position. To do that, your head must be in the proper

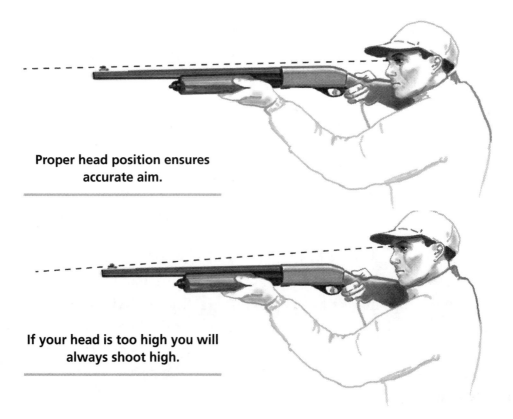

Proper head position ensures accurate aim.

If your head is too high you will always shoot high.

position on the shotgun and the butt of the shotgun stock seated firmly in your shoulder "pocket"—the soft area between your outer shoulder bone and your collarbone.

Here are the steps you should follow:

- Get in the ready position, with the barrel pointed in the direction you expect the target (bird or clay pigeon). Keep the butt of the gun tucked lightly under your armpit.
- Watch the target to see the line of flight. Don't hurry; you'll have more time than you think.
- Push the front end of the gun toward the target with your forward hand and into the target's flight path.
- Follow the target as if you were pointing your forward finger at it. Paint a stripe through it and keep bringing the stock up to your shoulder and cheek.
- Bring the stock to your cheek and into your shoulder at the same time.
- Pull the trigger, and your forward swinging motion will keep up with the target.

This motion is one smooth, flowing action.

Practice this swinging and shouldering motion with an unloaded shotgun again and again until it becomes a natural movement. It's the first step to becoming a good wingshot.

Positioning your feet right is important, too. If you don't have a stable, well-balanced stance, it's harder to swing the shotgun smoothly. This will cause you to miss more often.

The most effective shooting position is usually with your feet spread approximately shoulder width. If you're a right-handed shooter, your left foot and shoulder should be slightly ahead of your right foot and shoulder, toward the direction you're going to shoot. Your weight should be slightly forward and on the balls of your feet rather than on your heels, so you can swing the gun more easily. Don't lean so far forward that you feel uncomfortable and off balance.

When you swing the gun barrel, twist your upper body rather than just moving the gun with your arms. This also helps give you a smoother, steadier swing.

Getting Out in Front

In football, if you want to hit the tight end running a post pattern, you have to aim the ball in front of the receiver instead of directly at him. That way, the ball and the receiver will arrive at the same spot at the same time.

If you want to hit a flying duck with a shotgun, you have to do the same thing. You have to aim the gun at a point in front of the duck so the shot and the bird will arrive at the same point at the same time. This is called *leading* the target.

Swinging the gun through the target as you mount the gun will give you this lead automatically. Just keep the gun moving in a smooth swing; don't stop the barrel when you pull the trigger.

Walk Before You Run

Becoming a good wingshot isn't hard, any more than riding a bicycle is hard. It just takes practice. Probably the best way for a beginning wingshooter to learn the basics is by shooting several boxes of shells at clay targets.

You can go to a skeet range and do this. If you do, it's best to start with incoming clay targets. With the targets coming toward you, you'll have more time to react. The target becomes bigger the closer it gets and is therefore easier to hit. Going-away targets, on the other hand, could lead you to push the panic button and rush your shot.

Practice incoming shots until you start breaking clay targets regularly. Don't try learning it all in one practice session, though. Shooting one or at most two boxes of shotgun shells is plenty your first time out.

Light field loads or skeet loads kick less than heavy hunting loads and will save a sore shoulder after a day of practice.

Here's how to get started:.

- Watch the sky where the target is going to appear and wait for the target to come into your field of view.

- When you see it, begin your swing by bringing the gun barrel up along the flight path of the target and moving your gun barrel along the path until it catches up to the target.

- Bring the gun smoothly to your shoulder, the way you've been practicing. As the gun comes to your shoulder and your cheek finds its place on the gunstock, continue to swing the barrel by twisting your body and pivoting on the balls of your feet.

- Squeeze the trigger as the barrel covers the target, and continue the swing after the shot.

Remember, keep swinging the gun after it goes off and the shot is on its way. Stopping the barrel too soon is one of the leading causes of missing with a shotgun, and continuing the swing after pulling the trigger (this is called swinging through) is the surest way to eliminate the problem.

Playing All the Angles

When you are able to break these incoming targets regularly, try some of the other skeet stations and practice on going-away and crossing targets. These targets will be flying at a greater angle relative to your position, and you'll have to increase the amount of lead in order to hit them.

Don't panic. This is a lot easier than it sounds.

Remember that trick about starting your swing behind the target, catching up to it, and pulling the trigger when the barrel covers the target? It's the same thing all over again. Just bring your gun barrel along the flight path of the bird, swing through the target, and pull the trigger when the target disappears behind the gun barrel. This method automatically gives you the proper amount of distance in your lead for targets moving at any angle.

When you get comfortable with hitting targets at this new angle, have your helper move still farther away from you and a few more steps forward (but in a safe position). The angle for this shot will be even greater, and so will the necessary amount of lead.

Wingshooting is as simple as that. The more you practice, of course, the better you'll be, but anyone with the desire and a moderate amount of hand-eye coordination can learn to hit flying targets. Just concentrate on the basics.

- Get the barrel in the ready position.
- Keep both eyes open.
- Keep your feet spread and your weight slightly forward.
- Swing the barrel through the target.
- Mount the stock to your shoulder and cheek in one easy movement.
- Pull the trigger when the target disappears behind the barrel.
- Keep the barrel moving after the shot.

Hunting Tactics

Tall initial capital:

There are many ways to hunt ducks and geese successfully. The best tactics usually vary depending on the species you are hunting and where that species is found.

Some ducks—like teal, wigeon, and gadwall—inhabit shallow, weedy marshes and flooded fields. Wood ducks like woodland ponds, streams, and flooded woods. Pintails prefer big, open marshes and grain fields. Scaup, ringnecks, redheads, canvasbacks, and other bay ducks spend most of their time in open water on lakes and rivers. Geese and some dabblers spend a lot of their time feeding in agricultural fields. Mallards don't seem to have a favorite habitat. You might find them in any of these places.

Just keep in mind that time of day is important when hunting waterfowl. Ducks and geese move in the mornings and evening in search of food and cover. These are therefore the best times to hunt them, while midday is usually an unproductive time for most types of hunting.

Here are a few suggestions on how to hunt ducks and geese in places they are often found.

Hunting Marshes and Flooded Fields

The key to a successful hunt in both large marshes and flooded fields is staying out of sight.

In large marshes, you can often hide among the cattails or bulrush, or lean against a muskrat house to break your outline. Select an area sheltered from wind and waves—ducks and geese like to land in these quiet spots. You can also set up on points of land that stick out into the marsh or on islands

of cover. This allows you to intercept flying birds. Decoys, calls, chest waders, boats, and retrievers are usually important tools of the trade when hunting large marshes.

Flooded fields don't usually have much standing vegetation where you can hide. You will need a blind of some sort to hide from circling ducks. In shallow water, you can make a simple and effective blind by sticking two rows of cane or leafy branches into the mud about two feet apart and sitting on a five-gallon bucket. You must remain very still when ducks are working because they'll spot any movement through the thin cover of your blind. But if you don't move, a primitive blind like this is usually good enough.

You can also make blinds from camouflage burlap or other fabric attached to simple wooden poles.

Hunting Flooded Green Timber

Hunting flooded woods is the favorite method of hunting mallards and wood ducks for many hunters. It's mostly a southern hunting method, but

it works anywhere you can find flooded woods along a lake or stream.

It's a simple method of hunting. In most cases you don't need decoys or blinds in flooded timber. All you need are chest waders, a shotgun, warm clothes, and the ability to blow a duck call. You just sit on a log or lean against a tree and call to the passing ducks.

Hunting Dead-Timber Floodings

In ponds or sloughs with standing dead trees, you can sometimes simply lean against a snag or stump and hide from ducks. These places also often have brushy borders where you can hide.

Sometimes, though, the water in these flooded areas is too deep to wade, or the bottom is too soft. Hunting from a small, drab-colored boat is the answer to this problem. If the boat has an attached blind, you can set up just about anywhere, as long as you remain still when ducks are circling. If your boat isn't equipped with a blind, it's best to set up along the brush at the edge of the hunting area.

Be sure your boat doesn't have any bright-colored or shiny objects showing. Cover the gas tank and outboard with a camo or brown cloth.

Ducks use these dead-timber floodings as resting places. When there's a wind blowing, the best place to set up is usually on the upwind side of the opening in the timber. The brush and shoreline vegetation helps block the wind here and creates a quiet place that ducks will fly to.

Hunting Dry Fields

Dry grainfields can offer great hunting opportunities as well. In the early morning and late afternoon, ducks and geese will fly from their resting places to feed on the leftover grain in harvested fields. The key to a successful hunt is to find the spot where the birds will be.

You can do this by scouting. Drive the backroads the afternoon before your morning hunt (or vice versa), and look for ducks and geese feeding in grainfields. Once you find the birds, ask the landowner for permission to hunt.

Arrive well before dawn the next morning and set up your decoy spread. Large spreads are often used to attract the birds and to help you hide from them. Likewise, use plenty of goose decoys, even if you're targeting mainly ducks. These bigger decoys will help get your spread noticed and will be highly attractive to both ducks and geese.

You can hide among the decoys by lying on the ground or by using a portable blind. If you lie on the ground, it's a good idea to bring three things: a waterproof pad in case the ground is damp, a piece of burlap or camouflage material to pull over your body, and a camouflage facemask to make you even more invisible to the birds.

Hunting Ponds

Sneaking up on farm ponds or potholes and jump-shooting ducks as they flush is effective. The trick is get into shotgun range before the ducks see or hear you. The important thing is to stay out of sight and be quiet until you're well within range.

This is often easy to do because many ponds are small and surrounded by brushy shoreline cover. All you have to do is quietly sneak in behind the cover, get ready, and flush the birds.

On other ponds, you may have to sneak from one hiding place to the next, sometimes crawling on your hands and knees. If the pond has been created by a small dam, you can use the lower side of the dam as cover, walk up to the topside, and surprise the ducks.

Whichever method you use, keep your gun unloaded until you're ready to flush the ducks. Be sure to check your gun barrel for obstructions before loading it, especially if you had to crawl.

Float-Hunting Small Streams

Drifting in a canoe or small flat-bottomed boat is a good way for two people to hunt small streams. One person sits in the back and uses a paddle to keep the boat positioned. The other person sits in front with a gun. The hunters swap positions occasionally so both can share in the shooting.

A drab-colored boat is best for this type of hunting, and it sometimes helps to rig a small blind or pile of brush on the bow so you have something to hide behind as you approach ducks on the water. Be especially alert when going around sharp bends or where brush or shoreline vegetation extends into the water.

Talk in whispers, and don't make noise with the boat. Wear a PFD at all times and watch out for people and property as you move along the stream.

Jump-Shooting Small Streams

Another good way to hunt small creeks and streams is to walk along the banks. Use the vegetation and stream banks to hide your approach, and carefully slip into shotgun range of all sharp bends and brushy areas. It is usually more effective if you move into the wind because the ducks will have to take off toward you when they flush.

Sometimes two hunters can be more effective than one. One hunter should be on each side of the stream. As you work along the banks, approach each bend and brushy area at the same time. Often one hunter will flush ducks over his partner. Be careful where you're shooting, and never shoot at low-flying ducks when hunting with someone else. Be aware of landowner restrictions before you set out.

Hunting From a Blind on Small Streams

A wide place or a sheltered backwater off a small stream sometimes makes a good hunting spot. The best place to set up is against the brush or bank on the upwind side of the opening or wide spot. Place decoys in the open water in front of you. You can build a blind, hunt from a camouflaged boat, or stand at the edge of the water in the shoreline brush.

Small streams can be especially good hunting places when the weather turns bad. Ducks seek out these small waters because they provide shelter and because the moving water stays open longer late in the season when other waters freeze up.

Hunting Larger Streams

If the shoreline is brushy enough, it's sometimes possible to float-hunt larger streams and rivers from a boat. Jump-shooting ducks can also work well, and so does building a blind or hunting from your well-hidden boat anchored in sheltered areas of quiet water.

Pass-Shooting

Pass-shooting is one of the simplest methods for hunting ducks and geese. You don't need a lot of equipment, either, but you do need to find an area you know the birds will fly over. Observation and scouting will help you determine where these traditional flightlines are located. Then you hide and wait for the birds to fly within shooting range.

Other Methods

There are many other places and methods for hunting waterfowl, including large open water, where diving ducks and sea ducks are found. More information on these and other hunting techniques can be found in an excellent pair of Ducks Unlimited books, *A Ducks Unlimited Guide to Hunting Dabblers* and *A Ducks Unlimited Guide to Hunting Diving & Sea Ducks*, and in some of the other titles listed at the back of this book.

Calls and Calling

Calling is an important part of most waterfowl hunting. The better
you are at calling in birds, the more successful you're going to be.

The only times you *don't* need to call waterfowl is when you are floating
a stream and jump-shooting a farm pond or field where ducks and geese are
resting or feeding.

Calling works because waterfowl "talk" or communicate with each other
in order to attract mates or help flocks find food or avoid predators.

It's not difficult to learn how to blow a duck or goose call. But like
anything else, it takes practice.

There are several ways to learn calling. In many parts of the U.S. and
Canada you can find classes that teach beginning hunters how to blow a

call. You can also buy videos, CDs, or cassette tapes of duck or goose calling instructions. One of the best ways to learn is to ask a more experienced hunter who can call well to help you get started.

The most important technique in proper calling is to push air through the call with your stomach and diaphragm instead of blowing it through the call like you were blowing up a balloon.

It's a difficult process to explain, but it's similar to coughing. Once you learn to force air through the call this way, you'll start producing the raspy, deeper notes that sound like a real duck.

Once you've learned this trick, becoming a good caller is simply a matter of repetition and listening to yourself. The best way to hear yourself is to record your calling on a tape recorder and then play it back.

Practice as often as you can, even if it's only for a few minutes each time. Carry your favorite call with you and practice throughout the year, not just the day before the season opens. Listen to tame waterfowl at a park, zoo, or game farm to see how they sound and behave. It won't be long before you're sounding like a duck or goose.

The Sounds They Make

Most types of dabbling ducks will join flocks of mallards. And because mallards also have a loud call that carries well over a long distance, most duck hunters imitate the sounds of the hen mallard.

There are two basic types of sounds made by a hen mallard. These are the quack and the chuckle, also sometimes known as the feeding call.

To make the basic quack sound, say the word *quit* into the duck call in your deepest voice. This will help you bring the air up from your diaphragm.

By stringing several quacks together and varying their volume and tone, you can "say" different things to passing ducks. Each combination of quacks sends a different message.

The hail call, often called the highball, is a series of six or seven loud quacks made by the hen. Usually, the series of quacks tails off toward the end and the sounds get softer and calmer.

The lonesome hen call, which hens also use as a resting or assembly call, is a low, flat quack. It has less volume and excitement than the highball and can't be heard from as far away. The lonesome hen call is repeated two or three times over a span of five or six seconds. Don't make the quacks too close together, because if you do you're making the alarm call. Ducks make the alarm call when they're flushed from the water and are leaving as fast as they can. It's not a message you want to send to ducks you're trying to call in.

The chuckle is a much lower-volume sound than the quack. It is a muttering, chuckling string of rapid-fire single notes sounding like *tick, tick, tick, tick, tick,* or a two-note string of sounds like *ticka, ticka, ticka, ticka.* It's a call used by females in flocks or during courtship and so it's particularly attractive to males on the prowl for potential mates.

There are other calls that experienced hunters use—and sometime duck calls go by different names—but these will get you started. And a good tape or video will show you when to use them.

Try your calling with one or two of your hunting partners and together you can sound like a whole flock of birds. Practice using your hand to change the direction and tone of your calls and see how the birds respond to your special effects.

A Few Other Species

Here are a few other major waterfowl species in North America, along with the sound of the call used to bring them in.

- Wigeon: three-noted male whistle *whee-whee-whew*

- Wood Duck: *whoo-eek, whoo-eek, whoo-eek*

- Pintail: two-tone wheezy whistle *prrip prrip*

- Scaup/Redhead/Canvasback: guttural calls and growls, variations on *brrr-brrr- brrr*

- Canada Goose: *honk ka-ronk*

- Snow Goose: loud high nasal *houck-houck*

- Brant: throaty *krr-onk krr-onk*

- White-Fronted Goose: high-pitched tootling *kah-lah-a-luk*

What to Say and When to Say It

Learning to sound like a duck or goose is only part of being a good caller. Calling will grab the attention of passing birds, but your goal is to get them close so you can bring them cleanly to bag without crippling them. To do this you must learn which of the various calls to make and when to make them. For this, the best teachers are the ducks themselves.

In most cases, loud calling is the best option when you first spot a flock of ducks or geese and begin calling to them. That's why the highball is usually the first call hunters use when they start calling to a flock of birds.

Once the birds turn your way, most experienced hunters tone down their calling. They switch from loud, long strings of quacks to shorter, softer strings. When the birds are still 100–150 yards away, it's usually best to quit calling altogether and stay motionless, or to switch to a few soft chuckles as the ducks pass over.

After the birds are past you, start calling again with a loud but short highball. If the birds turn and head back your way, switch back to soft chuckles or quit calling altogether. If they pass overhead or off to the side and are still out of range, repeat the process.

Sometimes, though, this style of calling doesn't work. Sometimes the birds want a lot of loud calling, and sometimes the best calling is no calling at all. If what you're doing isn't bringing the birds in, try something different until you find what they like.

Remember, the best teachers are the ducks and geese themselves.

Decoys and Decoy Spreads

Ducks and geese have good eyesight, and at most times of the year they feel safer when they are with others of their kind. That's why in summer, fall, and winter they usually are found in small or large flocks. It's also why decoys are important for most types of waterfowl hunting.

Some guides on big lakes or open-water marshes and some southern goose hunters use more than a thousand decoys at a time. If you're hunting smaller waters, though, such as a quiet backwater on a stream, a small pond, or a pothole in a field or marsh, six or eight decoys may be enough.

The most important thing with decoys is putting them where they look natural, and in a place where ducks or geese will feel comfortable. If the wind is blowing, try to place your decoys in a sheltered place, because ducks usually try to stay in these sheltered spots when it's windy. If there's ice on the water, try to find a spot where current, a spring, or direct sunshine has kept the water from freezing. In some cases you may be able to break a bit of ice to make an opening. Ducks look for these places, too, and your decoys look natural there.

Some hunters have fairly good luck with old, beat-up decoys. Some duck hunters even use old plastic jugs painted to resemble the colors of ducks. In a pinch you can make crude decoy spreads by laying out white rags, newspapers, or even diapers in a dry field to attract snow geese, and black cloth or tarpaper to attract Canada geese and ducks. Add realism by positioning your set so it looks like they're feeding along the lines of grain swaths in the field.

All these things will work sometimes. But you'll probably have better luck if your decoys actually look like ducks or geese.

Types of Decoys

There are many sizes and types of decoys. You can get decoys made of solid foam that are very realistic looking and durable, but they're also expensive and it's hard to carry very many of them because they're bulky. If you have to walk very far to your hunting spot, other types of decoys may be better.

One of the most common types of decoys is made from hollow plastic. They are light and can be very realistic. Blow-up or self-inflating rubber

floating decoys are useful in remote places. Also recommended are soft-foam "half-shell" decoys, which have removable heads and stack together like cereal bowls. They're light and compact, and they're very good for hunting small potholes, beaver ponds, or other small waters that can't be reached except by walking.

For hunting in dry fields or along shorelines, some hunters use silhouette decoys. These are flat, cutout-type decoys made of heavy cardboard, thin plywood, or flat plastic that shows the profile of ducks or geese. These decoys are light and you can carry a lot of them with you. Set these at varying angles so that the birds you're decoying can see the set from all directions.

Decoys are also made from other materials, such as cork and wood, but these are usually more expensive. Making your own decoys out of simple materials is a great hobby and will reduce your costs. Look for places where you and your friends can sign up for a course during the winter, and by fall you'll have your own self-made spread of decoys.

Rigging Your Decoys

When you hunt over water, your decoys need lines and anchor weights to keep them from drifting away. Dark nylon cord is the best material for decoy lines because the ducks can't see it, it doesn't rot, and it's inexpensive. Brown insulated lamp wire is another great option. Weights can be almost anything that sinks and is heavy enough to keep a decoy in place. Many hunters use large bolts, railroad spikes, or old spark plugs. Some hunters use lead strap anchors molded into a thin bar about six inches long with a hole in one end. The lead bars can be bent and wrapped around the neck of the decoy when not in use, which helps to keep the lines untangled. Mushroom and scoop anchors are other designs you'll see at most hunting stores. Having the right rigging on your decoys will allow you to set them out and pick them up quickly, which you'll appreciate on a cold, windy day when the birds are really flying.

How long should the decoy lines be? That depends on the depth of the water you're hunting. In most cases, on small waters, three or four feet of line on each decoy will be plenty. If the water is deeper, of course, the lines must be longer. A good rule of thumb is to set your lines twice the depth of the water.

Setting Them Out

It is important that you put out decoys in a spread that looks realistic. The decoys should be positioned like a real flock of ducks or geese would be, and they should be in a place where ducks or geese would feel comfortable. Experienced hunters often go to a lot of trouble to set out their spreads just exactly this way or that way, particularly when hunting big water. But others aren't quite so picky.

The important thing is to make sure the farthest decoys are still within shooting range (less than 40 yards) of your blind or hiding spot so you can get birds in close, make clean kills, and avoid crippling loss. Waterfowl, like

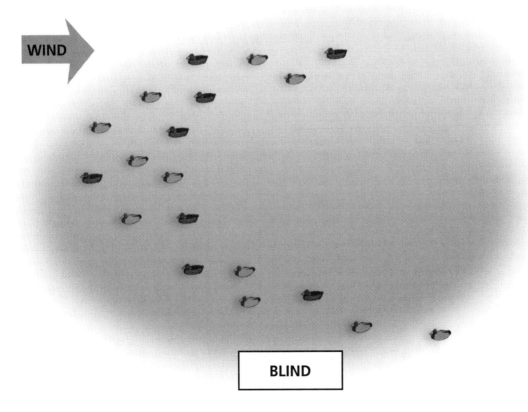

airplanes, like to take off and land into the wind, so take advantage of this in placing your decoys. With the wind at your back or side, face your decoys into the wind and leave an open space where waterfowl can land within gunshot. Don't let your decoys drift into each other and touch. Puddle ducks will usually pitch in behind the decoys, while divers will fly over or along the outside edge of the decoys and land in an opening at the front of the spread.

Adding Motion to Your Spread

Since real ducks move around when they're on the water, at least some of your decoys should move, too.

When there's a wind blowing, you'll often get enough motion from the waves as the decoys shift back and forth on the end of their cords. You need something more when it's calm and the water is flat and smooth.

In recent years, many manufacturers have built mechanical ducks of many kinds to add movement to decoys—flapping-wing or spinning-wing decoys, decoys with magnetic wobblers inside them, swimming decoys, and more. These mechanical decoys work well, but in some areas, they're illegal.

You can add motion to your decoys in some cases by simply kicking the water. Other times, you can tie a string to one or two decoys and run it to your blind, and you can make the decoys move by jerking the string. Logically enough, this rig is called a "jerk string." It's probably the oldest method of creating movement in decoys, and it still works as well as it ever did.

Some jerk string set-ups are elaborate, with the string tied off to a tree or heavy weight beyond the decoys and rigged with a bungee cord in the middle, with several decoys tied along the string. When the main string is pulled, the decoys move in one direction. When it's released, they move back the other way.

How you do it isn't important. What's important is that you make your decoys move when the weather is calm.

After the Hunt

Y ou've patterned your shotgun and practiced until you can hit flying targets. You've learned to blow a duck call and how to identify the birds. You've done your preseason scouting and found a good place to hunt. You've made a good blind and put out your decoys in a natural arrangement, and everything went the way it was supposed to. Now you're standing there with a pair of fat drake mallards in your hand. What do you do now?

With your birds headed for the table, it's important to take proper care of them. Ducks and geese are delicious when they're properly handled and cooked.

Because waterfowl are heavily feathered, they retain body heat for a long time after they're dead. Spread your birds out as much as possible so this body heat can escape. Taking some of the breast feathers off can help cool them down faster. Hang your birds up in the shade by their necks or feet and keep the flies away from them.

Before you begin the cleaning process, check your birds for any leg bands and report these to conservation authorities later. Try to identify your birds to species, sex, and age using feather and body characteristics, and record your information in a hunting journal. Also note the weather, hunting location, hunting partners, and any other memorable information and sketches you'll enjoy and learn from. When you're back home, check out the stomach and gizzard contents of your birds because you can learn a lot of interesting things that can make you a better hunter and conservationist down the road.

Some hunters enjoy plucking colorful feathers to use for hobbies like fly tying. You may even want to make a wing collection to improve your identification skills.

If you're planning to have a bird mounted, it's important to protect it from damage until you can get it to a taxidermist. Lay the bird aside and don't pile it up with other ducks in the bottom of your boat or blind. Smooth any out-of-place feathers if you can. One good way to protect a bird that's going to be mounted is to let it cool and then put it in a bread sack or wrap it in a mesh bag (an onion sack or the leg of an old pair of panty hose works well for this). Freeze the bird as soon as possible and take it to the taxidermist as soon as you can to prevent freezer burn.

Preparing Waterfowl for Cooking

Ducks and geese can be plucked or skinned, depending on how they're going to be cooked. Some damaged birds or those with too many pinfeathers can be breasted—which means cutting and pulling the breast free from the bones and skin. For roasting or baking, plucking is usually best because the skin and fat layer helps keep the dark meat from drying out during cooking. It's best to do this chore outside because feathers are going to be everywhere when you finish. For protection from infection, always wear rubber gloves in the cleaning process.

Birds can be plucked by hand or with a plucking machine. Either way, dry birds are easier to pluck. If you are plucking by hand, don't try to pull too many feathers off at one time. Grasp a few feathers between your thumb and forefinger and pull them out. Some people prefer to pull the feathers out in the direction they're growing, and some like to pull "against the grain." Both methods work, so try both and see which you like better. Leave the wings, legs, and head on the bird while plucking so you have something to hang on to.

Once you've plucked the feathers, the body of the bird will probably still be coated with a fuzzy layer of down. This down can be singed away with a small flame, such as a propane torch or candle, but be very careful and only do this with adult supervision. Do this outside, too, because the odor of burning feathers isn't pleasant. Some long-time hunters remove the last bit of down by dipping their birds in a pot of hot wax and peeling the coating off once it's hardened—something you might see in a fancy beauty parlor. If you try this, again you'll need help from an adult. After the bird's feathers are off, rinse it in cool water and then cut off the wings, feet, and head.

If you're going to fry the bird or use it to make soup or gumbo, you can skin it instead of plucking it. To do this, first cut off the wings, feet, and head. Next, pull a few feathers off the breast until you can see the skin. Then cut the skin along the length of the breast with a thin, sharp knife. Pull the skin away from the breast and around the back, working it loose as you go.

Removing the entrails and other organs of either plucked or skinned birds is messy, but easy. Simply cut a slit in the soft underside of the bird below the breast, reach in with your hand, and pull the insides out. Rinse the bird thoroughly with clean water to clean away the blood both inside and out.

Now the birds can be frozen for later use, if desired. To keep them from freezer burning, wrap them tightly in plastic wrap and then put them in a deflated resealable plastic bag. If you have more time and room, you can instead place each bird in a milk carton or other container and add enough water to completely cover the bird, and then place the container in the freezer. Label each bird with species and date for later reference when cooking. Ducks and geese are best if they're eaten within a few months.

Remember, if you have to transport your birds after they're cleaned, tag your birds with your name and license number and leave one feathered wing attached to verify bag and possession limits.

Cooking Your Birds

Cooking waterfowl can be a lot of fun once you get the hang of it. Only shoot as many birds as you and your family can use within the legal limits and don't waste birds by giving them away to someone who probably won't eat them.

The main thing to remember about cooking ducks or geese is that the meat is dark and already fairly dry. Don't overcook them. Using simple seasonings along with bacon and/or vegetables and fruits (apples, mushrooms, celery, pears, onions, and such) as a stuffing will keep the birds moist and tasty. It also helps to cover them with foil during the baking process.

Ducks and geese are delicious on the table if they're handled well in the field and cooked properly. Make sure both of these after-the-hunt jobs are done right, and eating the game you take can be an enjoyable and important part of the hunting ritual. It's a good feeling to sit down to a tasty meal that was produced by your skills as a hunter.

More information on the proper handling and cooking of waterfowl can be found in the DU books *Duck and Goose Cookery* and *Wild Feasts*.

Understanding Waterfowl and Conservation

12

The Basics of Waterfowl Biology

Separating the various types of ducks, geese, and swans is fairly simple. There are two major types of ducks—dabbling ducks (or puddle ducks) and diving ducks (sometimes called bay ducks). The tiny ruddy duck and another major group, the sea ducks, are often lumped in with the divers, while the wood duck is usually grouped with the dabblers.

Another duck type, the whistling ducks (or tree ducks), resemble and are actually more closely related to geese and swans. Two species live in the southern U.S. and Mexico—the black-bellied whistling duck and the fulvous whistling duck.

There are two species of native North American swans (trumpeter and tundra), and six species of North American geese (Canada, white-fronted, emperor, brant, snow, and Ross's).

Find a good field guide book (see "Suggested Readings" on page 93) so you can learn to tell these birds apart on the wing or in the hand. In addition to body color, you can use size, shape, wing beat, behavior, habitat preferences, calls, field marks, and distribution to recognize the species of most birds you'll see.

Good hunters know what they're shooting at before they fire the gun. And the more you know about the habitats and food preferences of birds you identify, the better hunter and conservationist you'll become.

Dabbling Ducks

Mallards are the most common and widely distributed of the dabblers, and indeed of all ducks. Besides the mallard and wood duck, there are eight other common North American dabbling species: American wigeon,

gadwall, green-winged teal, blue-winged teal, cinnamon teal, American black duck, northern pintail, and northern shoveler.

Three other dabblers are mostly non-migratory and live in the extreme southern part of North America—the mottled duck, Florida duck, and Mexican duck. Both drakes and hens (males and females) of all three resemble the mallard hen.

Dabbling ducks, as their group name suggests, prefer shallow water. They usually feed on or near the surface of the water, where they get to their underwater foods by reaching down into the mud or sediment with their necks and bills while remaining afloat. This is known as "tipping up." Most dabblers feed on seeds and other vegetable matter during

much of the year, but they also eat small aquatic animals (snails, minnows, insects, crayfish, etc.), particularly during the egg-laying phase, when hens need more protein and calcium. Dabblers use their *lamellae*, short tooth-like projections lining the bill, to filter out food, much like whales use baleen. The shoveler, with its wide spatula-shaped bill, is the ultimate filter feeder.

The legs of dabbling ducks are set farther forward than those of diving ducks. Because of this, dabblers can't dive as well as divers. However, they can walk better on land, and they can spring immediately into the air by pushing off (from water or land) with their wings and feet. (The wood duck, which is generally classified with the dabblers, is actually a perching duck. Its legs are set even farther forward, and it has a well-developed hind toe to help it grip and maintain balance on tree limbs.)

Diving Ducks

Canvasbacks, redheads, ring-necked ducks, greater and lesser scaup—these are the diving ducks, which spend most of their lives in fresh or brackish water. Sea ducks also use freshwater, especially during breeding and migration seasons, but most of them usually spend their winters in salt water. These include scoters, eiders, bufflehead, long-tailed ducks (also called oldsquaw), harlequin ducks, common and Barrow's goldeneye, and mergansers. Sea ducks don't mate or breed until their second or third year.

Diving ducks feed mostly by swimming down to their food sources, so they can feed in much deeper water than dabbling ducks. They are much more likely to feed on aquatic animals than are the dabblers, but for some, the tubers and leafy parts of pondweeds and other aquatic plants are favored delicacies. Most diving ducks usually feed in water from 3 to 25 feet deep, but some can go deeper if necessary. Some of the sea ducks, particularly long-tailed ducks, are deep-diving specialists, going down 180 feet or more. As a general rule, diving and sea ducks are clumsy out of water and don't often stray far above the shoreline except during the nesting period.

The Annual Cycle

Most waterfowl make their nests on the ground, in leafy or shrubby cover, almost always close to potholes, ponds, or lakes. There are, however, exceptions. A few species—the canvasback, for example—build nests over water. And a few others, such as wood ducks, goldeneyes, bufflehead, and hooded mergansers nest in hollow trees and will readily use man-made nest boxes where natural cavities are in short supply. Among the more unusual nesters is the harlequin duck, which nests next to mountain streams near turbulent rapids.

Some species of ducks (mallards, for example) begin to pair off as early as August and September. For others (such as canvasbacks) pairing does not happen usually until March. Almost all ducks of breeding age have paired off by the time they arrive on the breeding grounds.

Because the male ducks of a given species live longer and outnumber the females, the pairing process can result in major competition among males. In addition to aggressively fighting off other males, the drakes will use calling and displays of their brightly colored plumage to entice a hen into choosing them. Hens usually select a new mate each year, while geese and swans usually pair for life and stay together in family units over the winter months.

Because there's so much variation in the breeding, nesting, migration, and wintering habits of the many waterfowl species, it's not possible to discuss them all here. So let's look at the life cycle of the most popular, most well known, and most widely distributed of all the world's waterfowl—the mallard. Keep in mind that the life cycles of other waterfowl species differ somewhat (this is especially true of geese and swans). You can refer to *Duck Country*, by Michael Furtman, and some of the other references listed at the back of this book to find out more.

Spring: Mallards start leaving their wintering grounds in the south by early February. They push northward, closely following the thaw. Sometimes they push too far and have to retreat a bit when spring blizzards or lingering cold weather keeps things icy. The birds follow traditional migration corridors called flyways and stop at resting and feeding places along the way.

Along with pintails, mallards are usually the first ducks to arrive on the breeding grounds. Most of them arrive, even in northern zones, by late April or early May. The female mallard usually leads her mate back to where she was raised. Once they arrive, the pairs begin to disperse onto small territories, which the male defends from other mallards. Home ranges provide feeding, resting, and nesting areas for each pair.

Mallard hens begin to nest in April over much of the breeding range. The nest consists of a scrape in the vegetation, and the hen covers her fragile eggs with down plucked from her breast when she leaves each day to bathe and feed. This keeps the eggs warm and out of view from prowling predators. The number of eggs per nest varies, but the average is about nine; older, more experienced birds generally lay more eggs than younger birds.

The hen lays one egg per day, and doesn't start incubating the eggs until her whole clutch is completed. She sits on the eggs for about 25 days before they all hatch together.

Many duck nests never last long enough for the eggs to hatch. Predators such as raccoons, skunks, mink, ground squirrels, gulls, crows, cats, coyotes, foxes, owls, hawks, and snakes eat duck eggs, and sometimes predators catch the hen on the nest and kill her as well. Hens that survive nest predation may try to nest again, making as many as five renesting attempts before the summer season gets too short. Again, it is the older birds that are the most persistent.

Even when a nest of eggs hatches, the danger factor is still high. Those same predators like to eat ducklings, too, and now some fish and turtles can be added to the list of predators. As soon as the newly hatched

71

chicks are dry (within 12 hours of hatching) the hen leads them to water. This is a hazardous overland journey that may involve hiking up to a mile or farther.

In spite of predators, ducks beat the odds with sheer numbers. When moisture is plentiful on the prairies, and ducks have enough wetland and upland habitat, the birds can thrive and reach record numbers. However, poor habitat conditions and poor nest cover can increase the likelihood of predation, as well as the likelihood of disease. Lack of water and proper habitat is therefore ultimately a greater threat to waterfowl than are predators.

Mallard ducklings need no encouragement to enter the water and are good swimmers from the first instant. They feed mostly on small insects, bugs, and plant parts as their feathers and muscles grow. As they mature, though, they gradually begin eating more seeds and plant parts to build up the fat reserves they will need to take on their first migration. Ducklings keep their downy feathers for about 18 days and then begin a gradual growth of hard feathers. They can usually fly short distances by the time they're 50 days old, at which time they are fully free-flying.

Mallard drake in eclipse plumage.

Summer: During the early summer, when the ducklings are still flightless, the adult ducks also go through a brief flightless stage, when they shed their old, worn-out feathers including the large wing feathers that allow them to fly. This process is called molting. The adults are flightless for about three weeks during this time, when they have a temporary coat of brown, dull feathers, called eclipse or basic plumage. The dull feathers help the flightless adults hide and avoid predators.

Another molt brings the birds back into bright breeding plumage in time to begin the courtship process all over again.

Fall: In addition to being among the first ducks to arrive on the breeding grounds, mallards are also among the last to leave. Some mallards stay as far north as they can and still find food in the ice and snow. Other species, such as pintails and blue-winged teal, migrate early and winter along the Gulf Coast or farther south, in Mexico and Central and South America.

Migration patterns vary from year to year. In mild winters with little snowfall, mallards and other hardy species stay much farther north than usual. In severe cold weather, most of the continent's duck population east of the Rocky Mountains will go to the most southerly states and even to Mexico and the Caribbean Islands. On the West Coast, the primary wintering area for most species is the Central Valley of California and the west coast of Mexico, south of the Rio Grande.

Winter: Duck populations are highest right after the breeding season, when the young ducks are nearly full-grown. As they begin to migrate south,

the population gradually drops due to predators, hunting, accidents, and the hardships of migration. Disease, too, can take a major toll of birds, with avian botulism and cholera among the worst killers. Research on these and other mortality factors is important in establishing new forms of management to increase waterfowl survival.

Quite a few of the ducks in the fall population die before the next nesting season. Banding studies indicate that from 35 to 50 percent of the fall population usually die before spring. Hunting pressure is only one part of the equation; even without hunting many of these birds would die from other causes. The careful setting of bag limits and season lengths for each species takes these factors into account so that healthy populations are maintained from year to year.

Of course, each of us must follow all of the game laws and assist biologists and researchers whenever we can. But the laws alone are not enough. We must also develop our own personal set of ethics to guide us while we are out in the field. Remember, *conservation* is the wise use of resources to ensure their availability for future generations. It is your responsibility to learn as much as you can and to pass these traditions down to the next generation of waterfowlers so the birds we love will always be there.

Waterfowl in Jeopardy

When the European colonists settled North America in the early 1600s, they discovered an abundance of wild game. Elk were common throughout much of the continent and caribou ranged from the Arctic as far south as Maine, New Hampshire, Vermont, Michigan and Minnesota. White-tailed deer and black bears were everywhere. And waterfowl literally blotted out the sun on their migration and wintering grounds.

The new colonists were amazed. In Europe, game was scarce and all of it belonged to upper-class landowners. Commoners were rarely allowed to hunt. But in the New World, things were different. The settlers needed food and hides for clothing and shelter, and the animals were there for the taking.

There was so much game the pioneers thought there'd never be an end to it. How could just a few settlers with one-shot black-powder guns ever pose a serious threat to such an abundance of wildlife?

But the human population grew quickly, and new settlers started arriving from many other European countries. There were less than 500 European settlers in all of North America in 1620, but ten years later the number had grown to more than 3,000.

Within another 100 years, more than 200,000 Europeans were living in what would become the United States and another 30,000 lived in New France, which would later become part of Canada

While 500 settlers probably didn't have much effect on the abundant game populations, several hundred thousand settlers certainly did. And it just got worse. By 1750, the population was more than 1.5 million. By 1800, it was nearly 5.5 million.

Wildlife populations suffered. Unregulated hunting and fur trapping were partly responsible, but an even bigger reason was the huge loss of habitat that occurred as thousands of land-hungry settlers cleared the forests and grasslands to raise livestock and plant crops.

Big game was largely gone from the eastern United States and the most heavily settled parts of eastern Canada by the mid-1800s, but waterfowl populations were still mostly unharmed. This was partly because ducks and geese used marshy, swampy, or flood-prone areas that were of less interest to the early settlers, and partly because big game animals yielded much more meat than waterfowl.

Waterfowl habitat, however, didn't fare so well. By the late 1800s, the railroad era and the gold and silver booms had opened up the Far West and North to immigrants from all over the world. These new settlers quickly transformed the prairie landscape from grasslands and wetlands to croplands and pastures intersected with a network of trails and roads. Waterfowl habitat was now in trouble.

The Market-Hunting Era

By the mid-19th century, more people lived in cities than lived outside of them. But these city-dwellers still needed food and clothing, and wild game continued to be the most abundant source of meat and hides. The short-lived but extremely destructive era of the market hunter had arrived.

Because they were hunting for money and not for sport, the old-time waterfowl market gunners employed bigger, more efficient guns. The huge and now-illegal 8-gauge shotgun was a popular market-hunting tool, because as big as it was, a man could still fire it from the shoulder. Some market hunters used what were known as "punt guns" – basically long-barreled cannons mounted on small boats that could be maneuvered into position before firing. These guns were muzzleloaders that could fire large quantities of shot at flocks of ducks as they sat on the water. This was usually done at night, using lanterns to confuse and attract the rafting birds.

A well-aimed punt gun could kill a hundred or more ducks with a single shot, but even those market hunters who used conventional 10-and 12-gauge shotguns commonly killed 150 to 200 ducks a day for several months during fall, winter, and spring. The hunters packed the birds in barrels and shipped them to market, usually by rail.

For half a century, the hollow boom of the market hunters' guns echoed across Chesapeake Bay, the Mississippi River Valley, California's Central Valley, the freshwater marshes of Lake Erie, and the brackish marshes of coastal Louisiana, as well as in several marshes in Ontario and Manitoba. Millions of canvasbacks, redheads, black ducks, bluebills, mallards, and other ducks were taken each year by commercial

Punt guns were mounted on small boats.

hunters, with no bag limits and no closed season. They shot from the time the first ducks arrived on wintering, staging, or breeding areas, throughout the ice-free period.

77

The Growth of Recreational Hunting

In addition to the heavy pressure of market hunting, sport hunting gained popularity between 1865 and the early 20th century. Gentleman farmers and rich businessmen established hunting clubs and camps in prime waterfowl areas in southern Manitoba, the Great Lakes marshes, the wet bottomlands along the Mississippi River, and numerous places along the Atlantic and Pacific flyways. Localized gunning pressure by these clubs was high, and the use of conservation practices and ethical standards was limited.

Wholesale Habitat Destruction

This combination of heavy recreational and market gunning, along with widespread habitat destruction on both the nesting and wintering grounds, took its toll. All across the United States and Canada, duck and goose numbers fell rapidly.

In these adventurous, exciting days of the late 1800s and early 1900s, few people gave any thought to conservation. Vast forests were cleared, partly to provide lumber for houses and industry, and partly to open the land for farming. In many cases, the trees were piled and burned, just to get them out of the way. In the West, grasslands were converted to crops, and throughout the continent large tracts of wetlands were ditched and drained.

Although the colonists of the 1600s believed wild game was too abundant to be wiped out, by 1900 their descendants knew better. In fact, they believed just the opposite—that most wildlife species were doomed to extinction.

They had good reason to think so. The once-abundant elk, bison, and caribou herds were gone from large parts of their range, and many shorebird species were in real trouble. The passenger pigeon, once the most numerous warm-blooded animal on earth, was on the verge of its eventual extinction.

Many people were beginning to

think that ducks and geese would become extinct as well, or at least so rare that hunting them would be pointless. No one knew anything about wildlife management. Very few people thought wildlife could even be managed.

Fortunately, some people didn't think that way.

The Birth of Wildlife Management

The first official North American attempt at natural resources conservation occurred in 1871, when the U.S. Congress created the U.S. Commission on Fish and Fisheries. In 1887, the Canadian government passed the Rocky Mountains Park Act, and Canada's first national park was created at Banff, Alberta. Other conservation actions followed in the next two decades, and the conservation movement was launched in earnest when U.S. President Theodore Roosevelt took office in 1900.

Roosevelt was an avid hunter and nature lover. He knew wildlife populations were in serious trouble, and set about doing something about it. Roosevelt knew that protecting as much wildlife habitat as possible was important, and did everything he could along those lines.

Teddy Roosevelt and John Muir

Roosevelt established the first U.S. bird reservation in 1903, at Pelican Island in Florida. Before leaving office in 1908, he created 50 more. These bird reservations were re-designated as National Wildlife Refuges in 1942. Roosevelt also established national parks, four big-game refuges, and the National Forest Service.

In Canada, the trend was similar. In 1908, the Dominion Parks Branch was established as a unit of the forestry department, and since that time, 40 national parks and more than 1,700 provincial protected areas have been designated.

In the early 1900s, governments and a few concerned outdoorsmen had also started looking for ways to conserve waterfowl and other wildlife. In 1912, the Game Conservation Society was established. It was a forerunner of the More Game Birds in America Foundation, which eventually became Ducks Unlimited. The Audubon Society and the Wildlife Management Institute also had their beginnings in the early 1900s, and their efforts led to new laws protecting birds. A major breakthrough occurred in 1918, when Canada and the United States agreed on the Migratory Bird Treaty. Ducks, geese, shorebirds, and other migratory birds finally received the protection they needed. Mexico signed on as a treaty partner in 1936.

The Migratory Bird Treaty regulated waterfowl hunting seasons, outlawed commercial hunting, and banned the sale or trade of specified animal parts, including feathers and meat. Some poachers continued to hunt waterfowl commercially, but ducks and geese now had government protection from two countries. Most of the market hunting activity died quickly.

The Conservation Ethic

Theodore Roosevelt wasn't the only voice in this new conservation movement. John Muir founded the Sierra Club in 1892. Gifford Pinchot, Chief Forester of Roosevelt's newly-formed U.S. Forest Service, brought 193 million acres into the national forest system.

Pinchot believed in conservation as well as protection. "Conservation" means using renewable natural resources, but using them wisely so they can replenish themselves through growth and reproduction. "Preservation" means setting aside natural resources without using them at all. To make the whole thing work, both preservation and conservation must be employed.

Today we preserve key tracts of threatened wildlife habitat and those species that are rare or endangered, and we conserve the other natural resources and species that we depend on for our own survival and well being.

Gifford Pinchot

Pinchot's philosophy was to use natural resources "for the greatest good for the greatest number of people for the greatest length of time." It's that last part—"for the greatest length of time" —that is the biggest difference between the beliefs of the early settlers and the founders of the conservation movement. The early settlers gave little thought to the future. Roosevelt, Muir, Pinchot, and other early conservationists realized that if they didn't plan for the future, wildlife and wild places would disappear forever. These forward-thinking people formed the nucleus of the conservation movement.

But it took more than just regulating hunting seasons and saving wild places. Even after Canada and the United States started protecting and conserving vital habitats, wildlife populations continued to decline.

Clearly, something else was needed.

The Turning of the Tide

Establishing national wildlife refuges, national forests, preserves, parks, and other lands for waterfowl and other wildlife were important steps in saving wildlife in North America. Setting hunting seasons, bag limits, and harvest regulations on game species were also important. So was outlawing the trade in feathers, meat, and other wild animal products.

But conservationists quickly learned that most wildlife populations needed even more help. And so the science of wildlife management was born.

Aldo Leopold

There are many notable wildlife management pioneers, but probably the most influential of all was Aldo Leopold. A lifelong hunter and outdoorsman, Leopold worked for the U.S. Forest Service for 19 years. He became Professor of Game Management at the University of Wisconsin, and went on to become the first chairman of the university's Department of Wildlife Management. This was the first wildlife management school to integrate the studies of forestry, agriculture, biology, zoology, ecology, education, and communication.

Leopold is widely recognized as the father of modern wildlife management. The principles and techniques he taught in the 1930s and 1940s are still in use today. He is best known as the author of *A Sand County Almanac*, probably the finest collection of nature essays ever written. Leopold promoted the idea that a public "land ethic" was needed as the cornerstone of wise land use and conservation.

Until Leopold's time, most people thought the best way to increase wildlife populations was to control predators and limit hunting. Leopold and others realized that habitat was even more essential to building game populations.

At first, wildlife management was full of guesswork, trial and error. But slowly the knowledge base grew, and researchers began to build on each other's discoveries. New techniques were developed to measure the effects of management practices such as habitat enhancement and bag limits. One important technique was marking individual animals, which allowed researchers to keep track of those animals and learn more about habitat use, food preferences, mating behavior, movements, and mortality.

In the case of waterfowl and other birds, leg banding was one of the easiest ways to mark individual animals. Jack Miner was the pioneer of banding in the Americas. Miner founded the Jack Miner Bird Sanctuary in southern Ontario, in 1904, and banded more than 90,000 ducks and geese during his lifetime.

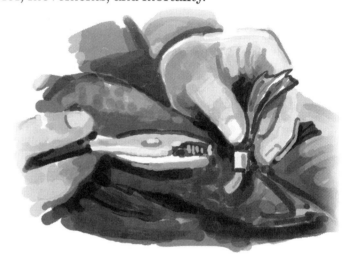

Putting a leg band on a duck.

To mark individual birds, researchers must be able to capture them and release them unharmed. Innovative capture methods include drive traps, flight nets, night lighting, cloverleaf traps, and decoy traps, which are actually reinventions of more primitive methods used centuries ago.

Hunters and other conservationists also play an important role in wildlife research by reporting sightings of marked birds and sending in information about their observations.

Much of the knowledge we have about ducks and geese today is a direct result of the things biologists have learned from studying the patterns and distribution of banded birds.

Putting Their Money Where Their Mouth Was

From the time the first so-called "game laws" were enacted, hunters have been buying hunting licenses and special permits. At first, these license fees were the only source of funding for most conservation and wildlife management programs.

In 1934, the U.S. Congress passed the Migratory Bird Hunting Stamp Act, which requires all duck and goose hunters to purchase a special stamp before hunting. The money raised through the sale of these stamps (commonly known as "duck stamps") is used to buy or otherwise protect important U.S. wetlands. More than 4.5 million acres of wetlands have been protected in this way. In 1985, similar legislation was passed in Canada.

Other U.S. legislation that proves hunters "put their money where their mouths are" is the Federal Aid in Wildlife Restoration Act (called the Pittman-Robertson Act), passed in

The first duck stamp was designed by Jay N. "Ding" Darling, who spearheaded passage of the Migratory Bird Hunting Stamp Act.

And Speaking of Hunters...

It may sound strange, but without hunters (and trappers, too), there would be less wildlife today. There would also be less incentive to study and conserve it, and less money to study and conserve it with. Teddy Roosevelt, Gifford Pinchot, Aldo Leopold, Jack Miner, and most of the other early conservationists and wildlife management professionals were hunters. When they saw things were getting steadily worse for wildlife, these men focused their passion for hunting on the struggle to save it.

That tradition holds to this day. Hunters continue to lend their support—in both time and money—to wildlife management research and on-the-ground habitat improvements.

1937. This act provides funding to restore and improve wildlife habitat and for wildlife management research, through a tax on hunting and fishing products.

To date, hunters have paid more than $5 billion into the wildlife fund, and that money has been sent back to the states to fund on-the-ground habitat work for all kinds of wildlife.

Under the North American Waterfowl Management Plan (NAWMP), launched in 1986 by an agreement between Canada and the United States (Mexico joined in 1988), major funding has gone toward habitat conservation work. These funds have come from the Pitman Robertson Fund, private sources like Ducks Unlimited, and special appropriations from state, provincial, and federal governments. The U.S. government's North American Wetlands Conservation Act of 1989 has been the main new mechanism to fuel NAWMP.

The North American Waterfowl Management Plan's goal is to return waterfowl populations to their 1970s average levels by conserving wetland and upland habitat. It is now considered to be one of the most ambitious and successful conservation initiatives in the world. To date, more than $547 million (U.S. dollars) has been invested through the Act. Total partner contributions have amounted to nearly $1.6 billion. Approximately 17.5 million acres (7 million hectares) of wetlands and associated uplands have been improved or protected across the continent. This provides tremendous benefits for waterfowl, other species and the environment in general.

The Dust Bowl Decade

The Migratory Bird Treaty and other improvements laid the foundation for bringing waterfowl populations back. But it soon became clear that much more effort – and more money – was needed.

The world's stock markets crashed in 1929, marking the start of the Great Depression. Thousands of people lost their jobs. Hunting license sales fell off. Then, in 1931, the worst drought in modern history hit central North America. From the Rocky Mountains to the Mississippi River and from Texas to Canada's Prairie Provinces, crops began to die from lack of rainfall and severe heat. This huge area came to be known as the Dust Bowl as the drought continued and got worse.

During the severe drought of the 1930's, huge dust storms devastated farmlands and livestock.

Thousands of farmers in the area went broke, abandoned their land, and headed west or to major cities in search of work. Livestock sickened and died, as did many humans in the drought area. Huge dust storms, known as "black blizzards," covered thousands of square miles and carried millions of tons of topsoil as far eastward as Washington, D.C. By 1934, when the first duck stamps went on sale, more than 135 million acres of U.S. agricultural land had been stripped of topsoil, and the topsoil was being rapidly blown away from another 125 million acres. The situation was almost as bad in southern Canada.

In the middle of all this human suffering, few people gave much thought to waterfowl. But the ducks were hurting, too. The Dust Bowl drought region overlapped much of the prairie pothole country of the northern U.S. and southern Canada, where most North American ducks are raised. The drought hurt duck populations in this area as much as it hurt farming. Millions of small potholes dried up completely, and most of the larger wetlands were devastated. This reduced the available nesting habitat, and duck numbers fell.

The Birth and Growth of Ducks Unlimited

During the decade of drought in the 1930s, the U.S Biological Survey, and the More Game Birds in America Foundation, headed by Joseph Knapp, realized that any program to increase waterfowl by improving habitat would have to be extended to Canada, where many of the birds nested. Because there was no mechanism for the United States to send public funds to Canada,

Joseph Knapp

private enterprise took over. Business leaders with an interest in waterfowl from both Canada and the United States met to develop a new partnership.

The partners ultimately agreed to establish a Canadian waterfowl restoration plan, including the creation of a non-profit foundation called Ducks Unlimited. The group announced the official incorporation of Ducks Unlimited, Inc., on January 29, 1937 and Ducks Unlimited Canada on March 10, 1937.

By the time the terrible drought finally ended in 1939, the U.S organization was actively raising funds and the Canadian group was conserving habitat. The first project was the restoration of Big Grass Marsh near Gladstone, Manitoba. The marsh was originally a 40,000 acre (16,000 hectare) wetland, but it had been mostly drained for agriculture between 1909 and 1916. Farming attempts were unsuccessful, and in 1938, DU Canada started construction of a water-management structure to restore the wetland. In 1942, Big Grass Marsh was at its peak water level, and the waterfowl population rose to the highest it had been since 1928.

Other DU projects swiftly followed across the prairies and into the north, and more and more hunter conservationists joined. By 1944, waterfowl populations rebounded, with the return of wetter conditions to the prairies, to their highest levels in 30 years. By 1950, DU and DU Canada had completed 307 projects, and by 1952 the total was 357.

In 1955, DU passed the $5 million mark for habitat-related expenditures in Canada, and over the next quarter century the tally rose to 1,718 projects totaling more than 2.8 million acres (1.1 million hectares) of wetlands. By 2002, more than $2 billion had been raised to conserve 11 million acres (4.5 million hectares) across the continent.

While Ducks Unlimited has remained focused on conserving wetland habitats, new programs continue to evolve. Until 1974 all fundraising was done in the United States, but that year the first fundraising banquet in Canada was held at Tilsonberg, Ontario. Until 1984, all DU habitat projects were in Canada, where most of North America's ducks nested. Beginning in that year, DU started funding wetland projects in the United States as well. New DU sister organizations were formed in Mexico (1974), New Zealand (1974), and Australia (1991).

Although there have been many ups and downs in waterfowl populations over the last seven decades, there's been much progress. Total spring waterfowl numbers remain near or above the long-term (1955 to 2002) average, and so do spring wetland pond numbers. However, a number of species still need help, and new research and recovery plans are needed. The work of Ducks Unlimited and like-minded organizations is as critical today as it was in the Dust Bowl era.

CHAPTER

15

The Future of Waterfowling and Conservation

A hundred years ago, waterfowl populations were shrinking rapidly. That was partly because ducks and geese were being harvested beyond their *biological limits*. But the main reason was because habitat was being destroyed to make way for houses, factories, and croplands. Unregulated pollution was also a big factor and so was erosion due to poor land-use practices.

Today, things have improved. We still have pollution, habitat destruction, and erosion, but we now know how to reduce and reverse some of these

91

impacts. We also have environmental laws that help businesses, governments, and people make the right environmental decisions.

Ducks Unlimited in the United States, Canada, and Mexico, and our partners, including private landowners, government agencies, corporations, and many other conservation organizations are working together to restore and protect wetland habitat for waterfowl and other living things, including people. Ducks Unlimited, for example, has protected or restored more than 11 million acres of wetland habitat across North America. State, provincial, and federal governments have also set aside millions more acres.

Despite this, more than half the wetlands in North America have been lost and many of those remaining have been damaged. Our wetland resources continue to be in jeopardy.

Much more effort and resources are needed to ensure the future of waterfowl and the future of waterfowling. Hunters continue to be the most dedicated conservationists by giving of their time, information, and hard-earned money to help the ducks. But more hunters need to think this way, and in some places there are fewer waterfowl hunters today then there were 25 years ago.

The steep decline in waterfowl populations has now largely been halted. North American duck and goose populations are relatively stable and the future for most species is generally bright. We'll always have problems with habitat destruction, drought, pollution, urban sprawl, and other things, but one thing is sure. With the growing effort and financial support of hunters and conservation groups, waterfowl hunting will continue to be a part of our heritage for a long, long time.

Suggested Readings

Batt, Bruce. *Snow Geese: Grandeur and Calamity on an Arctic Landscape.* Memphis: Ducks Unlimited, Inc., 1998.

Bellrose, Frank C. *Ducks, Geese, and Swans of North America.* Pennsylvania: Stackpole Books, 1981.

Bodsworth, Fred, W. S. Merwin.. *Last of the Curlews.* New York: Counterpoint Press, 1998.

Bourne, Wade. *A Ducks Unlimited Guide to Hunting Dabblers.* Memphis: Ducks Unlimited, Inc, 2002.

Bourne, Wade. *Decoys and Proven Methods for Using Them.* Memphis: Ducks Unlimited, Inc., 2002.

Robbins, Chandler S., Bertel Bruun, and Harold S. Zim. *Birds of North America: A Guide To Field Identification.* New York: St. Martin's Press, 2003.

Buckley, Bill. *Misery Loves Company: Waterfowling and the Relentless Pursuit of Self-Abuse.* Memphis: Ducks Unlimited, Inc., 2002.

Clarke, Eileen. *Duck & Goose Cookery.* Memphis: Ducks Unlimited, Inc., 2001.

Furtman, Michael. *Duck Country: A Celebration of America's Favorite Ducks.* Memphis: Ducks Unlimited, Inc., 2001.

Furtman, Michael. *On the Wings of a North Wind: A Journey with Waterfowl.* Adventure Publishers, 2000.

Gasset, Jose Ortega Y. *Meditations on Hunting.* Bozeman: Wilderness Adventures Press, 1996.

Kramer, Gary. *A Ducks Unlimited Guide to Hunting Diving & Sea Ducks.* Memphis: Ducks Unlimited, Inc., 2003.

LeMaster, Richard. *Waterfowl Identification: The Lemaster Method.* Pennsylvania: Stackpole Books, 1996.

Larsen, Doug. *Don't Shoot the Decoys: Original Stories of Waterfowling Obsession.* Memphis: Ducks Unlimited, Inc., 2002.

Leopold, Aldo. *A Sand County Almanac: With Essays on Conservation.* New York: Oxford University Press, 2002.

Michener, James A. *Chesapeake.* New York: Fawcett Books, 1986.

Miller, Stephen M. *Early American Waterfowling: 1700'S-1930.* New York: New Win Publishing, 1987.

Milner, Robert. *Retriever Training: A Back-to-Basics Approach.* Memphis: Ducks Unlimited, Inc., 2001.

National Safety Council. *Wilderness First Aid: Emergency Care for Remote Locations.* Jones & Bartlett Pub.,1997.

Peterson, Roger Tory. *A Field Guide to the Birds of Eastern and Central North America*. Boston: Houghton Mifflin Company, 2002.

Posewitz, Jim. *Beyond Fair Chase*. Connecticut: Falcon, 1994.

Reid, George K. *Pond Life: A Golden Guide*. New York: St. Martin's Press, 2003.

Reiger, John F. *American Sportsmen and the Origins of Conservation*. New York: New Win Publishing, 1975.

Wiseman, John. *SAS Survival Handbook: How to Survive in the Wild, in Any Climate, on Land or at Sea*. Lewis International Inc., 2003.

Zutz, Don. *The Ducks Unlimited Guide to Shotgunning*. Memphis: Ducks Unlimited, Inc., 1999.